# Learning to Walk by Grace

## A Study of Romans 6–11

# Bible Study Guide

From the Bible-teaching ministry of

## Charles R. Swindoll

discard

**Distributed by**

**WORD**

Educational Products Division
Waco, Texas 76796

INSIGHT FOR LIVING

Post Office Box 4444
Fullerton, California 92634

This guide is the second in a series of three study guides on the Book of Romans. These studies are based on the outlines of sermons delivered by Charles R. Swindoll. Chuck is a graduate of Dallas Theological Seminary and has served in pastorates for over twenty-two years, including churches in Texas, New England, and California. Since 1971 he has served as senior pastor of the First Evangelical Free Church of Fullerton, California. Chuck's radio program, "Insight for Living," began in 1979. In addition to his church and radio ministries, Chuck has authored twenty books and numerous booklets on a variety of subjects.

Chuck's outlines are expanded from the sermon transcripts and edited by Bill Watkins, a graduate of California State University at Fresno and Dallas Theological Seminary, with the assistance of Bill Butterworth, a graduate of Florida Bible College, Dallas Theological Seminary, and Florida Atlantic University. Bill Watkins is presently the director of educational resources, and Bill Butterworth is currently the director of counseling ministries at Insight for Living.

| | |
|---|---|
| **Publisher:** | Insight for Living, Fullerton, California |
| **Creative Director:** | Cynthia Swindoll |
| **Editor:** | Bill Watkins |
| **Associate Editor:** | Bill Butterworth |
| **Editorial Assistants:** | Jane Gillis, Wendy Jones, Julie Martin, and Karene Wells |
| **Communications Manager:** | Carla Beck |
| **Production Supervisor:** | Deedee Snyder |
| **Production Assistant:** | Linda Robertson |
| **Production Artists:** | Trina Crockett, Rhonda DiBello, Carla Randolph, and Jim Wikle |
| **Typographer:** | Trina Crockett |
| **Calligrapher:** | Richard Stumpf |
| **Cover Designer:** | Michael Standlee |
| **Printer:** | R. R. Donnelley & Sons Co. |
| **Cover:** | Painting by Homer Winslow, *Sunset, Saco Bay* |

An album that contains sixteen messages on eight cassettes and corresponds to this study guide may be purchased through Insight for Living, Post Office Box 4444, Fullerton, California 92634. For information, please write for the current Insight for Living catalog, or call (714) 870-9161. Canadian residents may direct their correspondence to Insight for Living Ministries, Post Office Box 2510, Vancouver, British Columbia, Canada V6B 3W7, or call (604) 669-1916.

# Table of Contents

Dying to Live .......................................................... 1

Whose Slave Are You? ............................................... 6

Portrait of a Struggling Christian ................................... 11

Free Spirit ............................................................ 17

Talking about Walking ............................................... 21

A Spirit-Controlled Mind-set ........................................ 26

The Glory and the Groan ............................................ 32

Providence Made Practical ........................................... 37

Providence Made Personal ........................................... 43

We Overwhelmingly Conquer ........................................ 47

God, the Jew, and You Too .......................................... 51

Straight Talk about Predestination .................................. 56

Straight Talk about Responsibility ................................... 62

The Jew: Cast Off or Set Aside? .................................... 66

Horticultural Ethics .................................................. 70

Unsearchable, Unfathomable, Unmatched! ........................... 74

Books for Probing Further ........................................... 79

# Learning to Walk by Grace

*It is doubtful that a more significant section of New Testament Scripture can be found than Romans 6–11. Who hasn't been helped by Paul's honesty in Romans 6 and 7? Who could ever measure the value of Romans 8? And where would we be without the insights in Romans 9, 10, and 11 regarding God's sovereignty, our responsibility, and Israel's destiny? These are powerful, life-changing truths!*

*Hopefully, this study guide will assist you as you work your way through the central core of the letter to the Romans. Be aware that this is not bedside reading for the casual Christian. You will need to concentrate as you follow the logic of theological thought. And for those of us who are diligent in our pursuit of truth, God will open wide the doors of understanding. Best of all, our walks will be affected!*

*Please pray daily for the Spirit to illumine your mind as you think God's thoughts after Him. Ask the Father to use each study to help you walk more consistently by grace.*

*Chuck Swindoll*

# Putting Truth into Action

*Knowledge apart from application falls short of God's desire for His children. Knowledge must result in change and growth. Consequently, we have constructed this Bible study guide with these purposes in mind: (1) to stimulate discovery, (2) to increase understanding, and (3) to encourage application.*

*At the end of each lesson is a section called* ![icon] ***Living Insights.*** *There you'll be given assistance in further Bible study, thoughtful interaction, and personal appropriation. This is the place where the lesson is fitted with shoe leather for your walk through the varied experiences of life.*

*It's our hope that you'll discover numerous ways to use this tool. Some useful avenues we would suggest are personal meditation, joint discovery, and discussion with your spouse, family, work associates, friends, or neighbors. The study guide is also practical for church classes, and, of course, as a study aid for the "Insight for Living" radio broadcast. The individual studies can usually be completed in thirty minutes. However, some are more open-ended and could be expanded for greater depth. Their use is flexible!*

*In order to derive the greatest benefit from this process, we suggest that you record your responses to the lessons in a notebook where writing space is plentiful. In view of the kinds of questions asked, your notebook may become a journal filled with your many discoveries and commitments. We anticipate you will find yourself returning to it periodically for review and encouragement.*

*Bill Watkins*
Editor

*Bill Butterworth*
Associate Editor

# Learning to Walk by Grace

## A STUDY OF ROMANS 6–11

# Dying to Live

*Romans 6:1–14*

In the first five chapters of Romans, Paul has laid the groundwork for the remainder of his epistle. He has established that every human being has fallen short of God's righteous standard. As a consequence, all are under the penalty of sin—which is everlasting death apart from God. However, man is not without hope. Rather than abandon him, the Lord has graciously paved a way for his rescue. When individuals trust in Christ's death on the cross as payment for their sins and believe that He rose from the dead to give them life, God will declare them righteous. In so doing, the Lord saves them from everlasting death and gives them everlasting life. For those who have embraced this gospel, a central question arises: Now that salvation from the *penalty* of sin has been received, how can salvation from the *power* of sin be secured? Being saved by grace is one thing, but being able to walk by grace . . . well, that's quite another. How can believers learn to live righteously? In the first half of Romans 6, Paul begins to tell us.

**I.  A Change in Management** (Romans 6:1–2).

The first step toward living the Christian life involves a believer's realization that he or she is dead to sin. Paul introduces this key thought by answering the objection of an imaginary critic. To the truth that we are saved by grace through faith, an objector could retort, "What shall we say then? Are we to continue in sin that grace might increase?" (v. 1). In other words, "Shall we who have been freed from sin still serve our old master as if we had never been emancipated?" "May it never be!" shouts Paul. "How shall we who died to sin still live in it?" (v. 2). Simply because the Lord has bought us out of the slave market of sin and set us free does not give us a license to do whatever we want. Through faith, we have passed from the old management to a whole new management headed by Christ. The sin nature that once ruled over us no longer has the power or authority to keep making directives in our lives. Christ has saved us from sin's penalty *and* power. Therefore, it would be a gross perversion of divine grace for us to continue to live as if sin were still our master.

## II. **Some Changes in Operation** (Romans 6:3–14).

Since we are dead to the power of sin, we need to live in light of that truth. But how can we gain control over a sin nature that no longer has any right to rule over us, yet continues to try to? These verses explain how we can experience daily victory over sin.

A. **What We Need to Know** (vv. 3–10). First of all, we need to realize that some truths apply to all Christians.

1. **We have been set free from sin through Christ's death and resurrection.** This fact is conveyed through three images. The first one is *baptism.* The text reads, "Or do you not know that all of us who have been baptized into Christ Jesus have been baptized into His death?" (v. 3). This is speaking not of water baptism but of spiritual baptism. The root idea is a change of identification. One who is saved by faith is not identified with sin any longer, but has a newfound identification with Christ. "Therefore," concludes Paul, "we have been buried with Him through baptism into death, in order that as Christ was raised from the dead through the glory of the Father, so we too might walk in newness of life" (v. 4). The triune God—Father, Son, and Holy Spirit—views the entire history of the universe from an eternal perspective. Everything is forever present in His sight. Thus, in the mind of God, when Christ died and rose from the dead, we who have trusted in Christ died and rose with Him. As far as God is concerned, salvation in Christ resulted in our dying to the sin nature within us and our living to the resurrection life of Christ (v. 5). In fact, "our old self [i.e., sin nature] was crucified with Him, [so] that our body of sin might be done away with [i.e., rendered inoperative], that we should no longer be slaves to sin" (v. 6). This imagery of *crucifixion* tells us that Christ's death on the cross covered our sin nature. Sin no longer has any power over Christians. It has been made ineffective. As a result, believers are now free from sin (v. 7). The shackles of *slavery* they habitually experienced have been broken. Christians do not have to serve sin ever again.

2. **We have been made alive to God through Christ's death and resurrection.** Paul makes this point very clear:

> Now if we have died with Christ, we believe that we shall also live with Him, knowing that Christ, having been raised from the dead, is never to die again; death no longer is master over Him. For the death that He died, He died to sin, once for all; but the life that He lives, He lives to God (vv. 8–10).

2

Since we have become identified with Christ in His death and resurrection, we have died to the sin He was crucified for and have been resurrected to the life He rose to give us. This new life is empowered by God for the overcoming of sin in every phase of our lives.

**B. What We Need to Consider** (vv. 11–12). Since it's an established fact that we as Christians have resurrection life and power, what do we need to do in order to take advantage of this truth? Paul answers us in these words: "Consider yourselves to be dead to sin, but alive to God in Christ Jesus." The Greek term for *consider* means "to calculate, take into account, figure." Through the use of this word, Paul is telling us to continually take into account that sin is no longer our master, but Christ is. Christ has freed us from the stranglehold of sin. We now have new life in Him and, through that life, we have the power to refuse sin's commands forever. "Therefore," writes Paul, "do not let sin reign in your mortal body that you should obey its lusts" (v. 12).

**C. What We Need to Present** (vv. 13–14). Up to this point, Paul has been dealing mainly with our self-concept. He has told us that we need to *think* of ourselves as under Christ's all-sufficient management. But what must we *do* to put this truth into practice? There are two steps we must take. The first one is negative: "Do not go on presenting the members of your body to sin as instruments of unrighteousness" (v. 13a). This passage assumes that we can quit sinning and calls on us to do exactly that. When we sin, the responsibility is laid at our doorstep. No one causes us to do wrong except ourselves (cf. James 1:13–15). And since we have the power through Christ to stop sinning, Paul exhorts us to plug into that power and quit performing unrighteous deeds. The next step is positive: "Present yourselves to God as those alive from the dead, and your members as instruments of righteousness to God" (Rom. 6:13b). That is, "Start living in a manner that manifests your right standing before God. Be Christlike in what you think, say, and do." The best defense is a good offense. And what better offense against sin than a godly lifestyle! Christ made it all possible by dying on the cross and rising from the dead for our sin. When we accept that fact by faith, sin ceases to be our master, and divine grace becomes the environment in which we live and grow (v. 14).

## III. A Response of Our Will.

During His earthly ministry, Jesus spoke these words:

"Truly, truly, I say to you, everyone who commits sin is the slave of sin. And the slave does not remain in the house forever; the son does remain forever. If therefore the Son shall make you free, you shall be free indeed" (John 8:34–36).

We who have found new life in Christ are free indeed. The problem is that we keep enslaving ourselves to our old master—sin. But we do not have to resubmit! Christ has broken our chains; He has secured our emancipation. Of course it may be difficult to overcome the control of entrenched, sinful habits. But we can do it by drawing upon Christ's resurrection power that is continually made available to us by the Holy Spirit. So let's begin *right now* to stop living as slaves to sin and start living as sons of God. Let's not put the process off any longer.

 *Living Insights*

**Study One**

For the serious student of Scripture, it is difficult to jump right into the middle of a book like Romans. Chapter 6 is exciting, but it is even more so when understood in the context of chapters 1–5. Let's do some *review* of where we've been so far.

- Take a few minutes to read Romans 1–5. After each chapter, stop and write down three or four *summary statements* that capsulize the chapter. This process will help you clarify your thoughts on these crucial sections of Romans.

| Chapters | Summary Statements |
|---|---|
| 1 | |
| 2 | |
| 3 | |
| 4 | |
| 5 | |

4

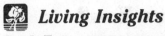 *Living Insights*

Summarizing chapters can be an excellent method of getting a grip on the truths set forth in this magnificent letter. So let's turn our attention from review to *preview*.

- Read Romans 6–11. After completing each chapter, take a few minutes to collect your thoughts by writing down three or four *summary statements*. You may want to note *questions* that arise during your reading. It's our hope that many of these questions will be answered during our time of study in this series.

| Chapters | Summary Statements | Questions |
|---|---|---|
| 6 | | |
| 7 | | |
| 8 | | |
| 9 | | |
| 10 | | |
| 11 | | |

5

# Whose Slave Are You?

*Romans 6:15–23*

Even if we are free in some respects, we can be enslaved in others. For instance, we can be enslaved to a job. Workaholics are prime examples of this kind of slavery. We can also become shackled by the things we own, or those goods we would like to possess. This master is materialism. If we have an inordinate desire to gain the approval of others, then we have become a slave of people. It is also possible to be in bondage to ourselves. Our own attitudes, prejudices, feelings, thoughts, and habits can ensnare us in a downward spiral of misery and helplessness. Is there anyone who can free us from these detrimental masters? The Apostle Paul answers with a resounding yes. He shows us how we can experience freedom from sin as we begin to practice our freedom in Christ.

## I.   Christians are free from sin.

Before we examine the last half of Romans 6, let's get a handle on the context by reviewing the first part of the chapter. In verses 1–14, Paul basically teaches that Christians have been freed from the slavery of their sin nature. That strong inborn desire to sin no longer has any right to rule over them. Therefore, Christians do not need to resubmit to their old master. Indeed, they should not yield to sin anymore but should submit themselves to God and live righteously. Paul develops this thought in three steps. First, he reminds believers of what they should *know*—namely, that when they believed in Christ's death and resurrection by faith, they were freed from sin to live forever in Christ (vv. 3–10). Second, believers should *consider* their newfound freedom as fact and act accordingly (v. 11). Third, Christians should stop submitting to sin and start *presenting* themselves to God as emancipated people (vv. 12–14). In short, Christians do not need to live like non-Christians, since they are under new management. Thus, they should obey their new Head and disregard their old one.

## II.   Christians are free from sinning.

In verses 15–21, Paul directs his attention from the root of sin to the fruits of sin, from the sin nature to sinful acts. In the first several verses of chapter 6, he answered no to the question, "Shall we sin in order to obtain grace?" As we approach the closing verses of this chapter, we find him addressing a similar question. This one is also asked as an objection to his teaching that justification comes by faith alone. "What then? Shall we sin because we are not under law but under grace?" (v. 15a). Paul answers, "May it never be!" (v. 15b). How foolish to think that being saved by God's grace could be construed as a reason for living as if we had not been saved! We have a new Master who is holy and righteous. He expects us to live in a manner that honors and reflects His character. He did not save us from sin so that we could continue sinning. Rather, He set us free from sin so that we could enjoy a godly life in His service. "But" we might ask, "how can we experience freedom from sinning? How can we serve God instead of sin on a day-to-day basis?" Paul tells us by presenting a universal principle to understand, a past condition to recall, a present choice to make, and an everlasting benefit to consider.

**A. A Universal Principle** (v. 16). Paul conveys it in these words: "Do you not know that when you present yourselves to someone as slaves for obedience, you are slaves of the one whom you obey, either of sin resulting in death, or of obedience resulting in righteousness?" The basic truth presented is this: *Obedience results in slavery.* Ultimately, there are only two masters we can choose to obey—sin or the Lord. When we yield to the directives of our sin nature, we are not simply sinning, but we are developing sinful habits. Thus, our obedience to sin enslaves us to a lifestyle that leads only to death. The *death* spoken of here is alienation from God. When we disobey the Lord, we do not lose our salvation, but we sever our fellowship with Him. This results in a loss of blessing, joy, peace, spiritual growth, and a clear conscience. It also leads to more wrongdoing, unless we turn to God in genuine repentance and thereby restore fellowship with Him (1 John 1:7–9). Of course, we can avoid all of this if we will choose to obey God. And when we do submit to His counsel, we begin to develop habits of holiness that will lead to further purity in our behavior.

**B. Our Past Condition** (vv. 17–19a). Before we became Christians, Paul reminds us again that we were "slaves of sin" (v. 17a). We became sin's obedient servants in at least two ways. First, we were born with an innate propensity toward a wrongful lifestyle. We did not actually choose to be born this way; we were conceived in this sinful state as the result of God's judgment on Adam's original act of disobedience (Gen. 2:16–17, 3:1–21; Rom. 5:12–21; Ps. 51:5). However, this sin nature did not cause us to sin, but it did make it easier—even more natural—for us to rebel against God. Second, the actual evil acts we committed drove us into a deeper subjection to sin. Paul makes this point when he states that as unbelievers we presented ourselves "as slaves to impurity and to lawlessness, resulting in futher lawlessness" (Rom. 6:19a). In summary, then, we were enslaved to sin *involuntarily,* in that we were born with a bent toward serving sin. And we were enslaved to sin *voluntarily,* in that we freely chose to submit to the sin nature within us.

**C. Our Present Choice** (vv. 17–20). But now we have been set free from our bondage to sin through our faith in Christ's atoning work. The Lord has made us new creatures (2 Cor. 5:17) who are free to be "slaves of righteousness" (Rom. 6:18). So why are we not habitually committed to a godly lifestyle? Why is it so difficult for us to consistently walk by grace? The answer to both questions is twofold. In the first place, *until we are raptured or resurrected, we will not be rid of our sin nature.* Although it no longer has any authority over us, it still raises its ugly head and tries to reenlist our servitude. In the second place, *our salvation from sin has given us the freedom and desire to live righteously, but it does not force us to do so.* We can still obey sin's commands, even though there is no need or necessity for us to do so. That's why Paul exhorts us to present ourselves "as slaves to righteousness, resulting in sanctification" (v. 19b). When we come to those daily forks in the road with one path labeled Right and the other one marked Wrong, the Lord calls on us to make the right choice. And through the power of His Holy Spirit, He gives us the strength to carry through with our decision to do what is good.

**D. Our Everlasting Benefit** (vv. 21–23). Paul wraps up his instruction by showing the contrast in benefits between serving sin and serving God. He begins with these words: "Therefore what benefit were you then deriving from the things of which you are now ashamed?" (v. 21a). Of course, the expected answer is that there were no blessings attached to our servitude under sin. In fact, *death* is the end result of such a lifestyle. Even believers who live unrighteously experience, in this life only, a type of death—namely, alienation and discipline from God. (cf. 1 Cor. 11:17–22, 27–32; James 5:19–20; 1 John 5:16). However, with respect to unbelievers, death encompasses separation and judgment from God both now and forever. On the other hand, service to God will bring *sanctification*—namely, a consistent walk with Christ that has holiness as its goal (cf. 1 Pet. 1:14–16, Jude 24). The consequence of this benefit is everlasting life (Rom. 6:22). This kind of life does not begin after death, but it becomes ours forever at the moment we put our trust in Jesus Christ as Savior (v. 23b). What greater motivation do we need to begin and persevere in a pursuit of holiness?

**III. Christians are free to learn from what they know.**
Among the several lessons we could draw from these verses, two are central.

**A. It's possible to be free, yet still live like we're enslaved.** Christians realize intellectually that sin is no longer their master, but they can behave experientially as if the opposite were true. If you are a believer in Christ, don't allow yourself to fall prey to this trap. God has given you the freedom and the power to be Christlike. Commit yourself today to begin developing habits of holiness.

**B. It's possible to be enslaved, yet still think that we're free.** This could only be true of non-Christians. If you have not trusted in Christ as your Savior, then don't be deceived. You are not free to become all God created you to be until you change masters. Please do not continue on your present path. Your servitude to sin has no real benefits and will lead to only one ultimate end—everlasting destruction. God desires to give you both freedom from sin and all the riches of everlasting life. To receive them, all He asks you to do is to accept His free gift of salvation in Christ by faith alone.

 *Living Insights*

**Study One**

Obedience results in slavery. We can be in bondage either to sin or to righteousness. Let's look more closely at this issue.

* Copy the following chart into your notebook. Reread Romans 6:15–23. In the left column, write down all the observations you make on *slavery to sin.* Use the right column for recording your observations on *slavery to righteousness.* Be thorough in your study, and be as specific as possible.

| Obedience Results in Slavery—Romans 6 | |
|---|---|
| Slavery to Sin | Slavery to Righteousness |
| | |

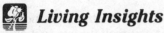 *Living Insights*

For those of us who are Christians, it's a sobering fact to realize that we can be free and yet be enslaved. Let's personalize this truth.

- You need to do something about sin. You can rely on the corrective theology of 1 John 1:9, or you can attempt to apply the preventive theology from Romans 6. Christ is already victorious; thus, the decision for victory is up to *you*. Take this time to honestly answer the following questions: How am I demonstrating slavery to righteousness? What am I doing to bring myself closer to the standard of righteousness?

# Portrait of a Struggling Christian

*Romans 7:1–24*

Romans 5:12–6:23 presents what appears to be an airtight case for living the Christian life *perfectly.* Relieved from the demands of the Law and released from the dominion of the sin nature, Christians seem to have all that they need to walk consistently with the Lord. But the honest truth is that we do still sin. In fact, even though we might want to, we can never perfectly obey God on our own. In Romans 7, the Apostle Paul admitted that he also personally struggled with wrongdoing. We can learn from his experience that this battle does not have to end in despair. Indeed, it should cause us to become refreshingly realistic.

## I. Positionally, Where We Stand.

We will not be able to evaluate and handle our struggle with sin without an understanding of our position in Christ. So let's consider Paul's words about this in Romans 6:1–7:13.

**A. The Sin Nature** (6:1–23). These verses announce the wonderful news that our salvation has set us free from sin and has given us new life in Christ. No longer do we have to obey the dictates of our old master, but we are now free to serve God through a righteous lifestyle.

**B. The Mosaic Law** (7:1–13). How does the Old Testament Law relate to our new position in Christ? In answer to this question, Paul uses an analogy drawn from marriage and civil law.

    **1. An Analogy** (vv. 1–3). The verses read as follows:

> Or do you not know, brethren (for I am speaking to those who know the law), that the law has jurisdiction over a person as long as he lives? For the married woman is bound by law to her husband while he is living; but if her husband dies, she is released from the law concerning the husband. So then if, while her husband is living, she is joined to another man, she shall be called an adulteress; but if her husband dies, she is free from the law, so that she is not an adulteress, though she is joined to another man.

    **2. The Application** (vv. 4–6). Just as death breaks the bond between a husband and a wife, so the believer's identification with Christ's death breaks the bond that yoked him to the Law. This Law required perfection. But because we failed to meet its standard, we stood condemned. However, through trusting in Christ's payment for sin, we died to the Law's jurisdiction over us. We have been released from our marital union with the Law and

11

have entered into a new marriage with Christ. As His bride, "we serve in newness of the Spirit and not in oldness of the letter" (v. 6).

3. **Some Benefits** (vv. 7–13). Someone could object to this teaching on the grounds that it implies the Law is sinful. To this fallacious charge Paul says, "May it never be!" (v. 7a). In fact, the Law is not only holy, but it has served three beneficial functions. The first one is that *the Law has defined sin* (v. 7b). It has clearly established what is wrong and right. In so doing, it has declared the righteous standard of God and revealed what falls short of it. Second, *the Law has provoked sin* (vv. 8–12). That is, the Law did not cause anyone to disobey God, but it aroused their inborn desire to sin. This brings us to the third benefit—namely, *the Law has exposed the cause of sin* (v. 13). God's Law does not force an individual to do anything. It simply sets forth the divine standard of righteousness, the blessings that will flow to those who obey it, and the cursings that will fall on those who disobey it. The responsibility for sin falls on man who has willingly submitted to his sin nature rather than the holy dictates of the Law. In summary, the Law has served its primary purpose: to reveal man's desperate need for God's abundant grace.

## II. **Experientially, Why We Struggle.**

If we are dead to our sin nature and to the Law's demands, then why do we have such a difficult time obeying God? Why can't we be consistently Christlike? This is not a new struggle; it is one that Paul wrestled with also. Indeed, he exclaimed in verse 24, "Wretched man that I am! Who will set me free from the body of this death?" Not even Paul, the zealous apostle and evangelist of our Lord, experienced a life free from struggle with sin. Why? Paul tells us in the verses that follow. What he says has a poignant relevance to our daily battle with disobedience.

A. **Facts to Face.** Paul gives us three facts that we must accept in our struggle with sin. The first one is conveyed in these words: "For we know that the Law is spiritual; but I am of flesh, sold into bondage to sin" (v. 14). In other words, *we cannot curb disobedience on our own.* The sin nature within each of us vies for control, prodding us into unrighteous acts. We might experience temporary victories over this enemy, but we will never conquer it by drawing on our own strength. The second fact we need to face is that *we do not fulfill our wishes.* Paul is very honest about this: "I am not practicing what I would like to do, but I am doing the very thing I hate . . . For I know that nothing good dwells in me, that is, in my flesh; for the wishing is present in me, but the doing of the good is not. For the good that I wish, I do not do; but I practice the very evil that I do not wish" (vv. 15b, 18–19). Why do we often fail to satisfy our desires to do good? The answer to this brings us to the third fact: *we dare not ignore our sin nature* (v. 17), for it actively promotes disobedience to God. And though it has no more valid authority over us, our sin nature still clamors for its old rule. If we fail to come to terms with this reality, then we are doomed to frustration and disillusionment in our Christian lives.

**B. Truth to Admit.** These certain facts point to two disturbing but biblical truths. First, *there is a civil war occurring within each of us* (vv. 17, 20, 22–23). Although we are new creatures in Christ and therefore possess a new drive to please God, we still have an old nature that is bent toward turning us against the Lord. The presence of these two natures creates an internal battle with each side striving for our attention and obedience. Second, *this civil war will not end until we are glorified.* Like a parasite, evil dwells in each of us and tries to suck away our desire to be godly. Not until our death or rapture will we finally experience *full* freedom from the power sin tries to exert over us. At that wonderful moment, we will stand holy and blameless in God's presence (Rom. 8:30, 1 Cor. 15:51–57, Jude 24).

**C. Results to Accept.** Two consequences that we need to acknowledge are suggested in these words:

For I joyfully concur with the law of God in the inner man, but I see a different law in the members of my body, waging war against the law of my mind, and making me a prisoner of the law of sin which is in my members. Wretched man that I am! Who will set me free from the body of this death (Rom. 7:22–24)?

*When we try to fight sin in the flesh, we lose.* We cannot have victory in our struggle if we draw only from ourselves. Furthermore, *when we focus on the flesh, we quit.* If we try to overcome sin on our own, then we will eventually become disillusioned and give up the fight.

## III. Realistically, How We Can Survive.

There is no quick and easy formula we can embrace that will resolve our conflict with sin. However, Romans 7 does provide some realistic strategy we can apply in this battle of wills.

**A. We should freely admit our own lack of understanding.** The Apostle Paul was able to say, "For that which I am doing, I do not understand; for I am not practicing what I would like to do, but I am doing the very thing I hate" (v. 15). He didn't always know why he failed to consistently please God. And he did not try to give people the impression that he was without problems. We would do well to model this kind of honesty before one another. Then we will discover the support from each other we need to carry on the fight.

**B. We should accept our own imperfections.** Paul knew that he was saved, but he also realized that he still sinned. This did not make him complacent in his struggle against sin, but it did breed a realistic approach to life that even brought contentment in the midst of extreme adversity (Phil. 4:11–13; cf. 2 Cor. 11:23–30). The same benefit can be ours if we will begin by acknowledging our own sinfulness and inadequacy.

**C. We should leave room for failure.** It's quite easy for us to handle personal victory, but defeat is a different matter. We don't want to face it, much less talk about it. But if we fail to realize that defeats will come, we will place unrealistic expectations on ourselves that can only lead to frustration and pessimism. God does not hate failure. After all, He loved failures so much that He sent His only Son to die for them. The Lord simply asks that we learn from our mistakes and use them to move closer to Him.

**D. We should admit our true feelings to God.** Paul was able to acknowledge his struggle with sin. Similar confessions can be found throughout Scripture, especially the Psalms (e.g., Pss. 32, 51). The Lord wants us to unload our true feelings on Him. When we do, we will find comfort and peace (cf. Matt. 11:28–29).

*Living Insights*

Because we usually don't think of people like the Apostle Paul struggling with sin, we often have trouble admitting our own struggles with it. Too many times our unrealistic ideas of the spiritual life cause us to think that we should be perfect. May Romans 7 be an encouragement to all who suffer with this idealistic approach to Christian living.

● Let's allow Paul's struggle in Romans 7 to be our own. Take the twenty-five verses of this chapter and write them out *in your own words.* However, let's be sure to compose this paraphrase in the first person. Thus, when you say, "I want to do good, but I just don't do it," you'll be personalizing this tension in your life. Be careful. This exercise is going to be incredibly convicting!

 *Living Insights*

This message will change your life . . . if you allow it to do so! The key is applying the truth that's been taught. So copy the charts that follow and fill in personal examples of current confusions, persistent imperfections, troubling failures, and honest emotions. Don't hold back. This stuff is too important to brush away quickly.

Freely say "I don't understand."

Accept your own imperfections.

Leave room for failure.

Admit your true feelings, especially to God.

# Free Spirit
*Romans 7:24–8:4*

"It's always darkest before the dawn." That saying is more often true than not. It certainly applies to the flow of Paul's thought in Romans 7–8. Chapter 7 is dark, heavy, and discouraging. It even climaxes with the gutteral groan of a saved sinner: "Wretched man that I am!" (v. 24a). But chapter 8 ushers in a dawn of welcomed hope and divine help. If you feel defeated in your struggle with sin, don't despair! God has not abandoned His people. In fact, He has given them the resources they need to become free spirits of grace, even in the midst of the fray.

**I. The Struggle Recalled** (Romans 7:14–24).

In order to appreciate the light God provides, let's briefly review the darkness we experience in our conflict with sin.

**A. Admissions.** Paul's struggles as a believer are reflective of ours as well. Like him, we often experience *confusion* because we find it so easy to go against our strong desires to do what is right (vv. 15, 19, 22–23). Of course, this reveals both our *imperfections* and our internal *battle* with sin (vv. 15, 17–18, 21–23). Because these factors apply to all believers, we are only fooling ourselves when we fail to admit them and pretend we are perfect. Indeed, this unbiblical response only reinforces the intensity of our struggle with sin.

**B. Emotions.** Our bout with sin produces several negative emotions. We can see four of them tucked away in Romans 7:24.

**1. "I am tired."** This feeling is conveyed in the Greek word for *wretched.* It means "to bear a callous." The term suggests working to the point of exhaustion. We can try all types of techniques and take various human avenues to produce the perfect Christian life, but we will only make ourselves weary in the process.

**2. "I am hopeless."** Out of exasperation, Paul asked, "Who will set me free?" He knew that his attempts to live righteously had failed. Indeed, they revealed how sinful he really was. In the same way, when we attempt to attain godliness on our own, the end result will be a sense of hopelessness.

**3. "I am trapped."** Paul's desire to be set free implied that he felt entrapped. Like us, he had died to the authority of his sin nature, but he could not break away from its grasp. Salvation from the penalty of sin was his; however, he had yet to experience salvation from sin's power.

4. **"I am condemned."** Paul desperately wanted to know how he could be released from "the body of this death." He felt condemned to live a life of defeat. How many times have we had the same feeling!

## II. Some Relief Expressed (Romans 7:25).

If Paul had ended in verse 24, we would have been left with a bleak picture of the Christian life. But he didn't stop there. He immediately moved on and closed chapter 7 with some words of hope. He begins verse 25 with an exclamation of gratitude: "Thanks be to God through Jesus Christ our Lord!" For what is he giving thanks? Certainly not for his wretchedness, but for what he unveils in chapter 8—namely, that *only God can bring relief to a believer's struggle with sin.* This fact logically leads Paul to make the following confession: "So then, on the one hand I myself with my mind am serving the law of God, but on the other, with my flesh the law of sin." Put another way, *believers cannot handle the struggle with sin on their own.* Their walk by grace must be God-dependent, not self-dependent.

## III. Several Answers Provided (Romans 8:1–4).

Paul presents us with two major resources that we can depend on the Lord to supply: encouragement for the discouraged and help for the helpless. Let's take a closer look at each one.

A. **Encouragement from God.** The Lord provides it in response to the four common emotions we experience in our daily battle with sin.

1. **"Do you feel condemned?"** Whenever we do, we should recall that "there is therefore now no condemnation for those who are in Christ Jesus" (v. 1). We do not have to feel put down or insecure in our spiritual struggles. Because we have been declared righteous through our faith in Christ, the Heavenly Father has wiped our slate clean of the penalty of sin.

2. **"Do you feel hopeless?"** This destructive emotion can be combatted by realizing that we are—*right now*—uncondemned by God (v. 1). We have a hope made certain by God's unchanging promise that He will never forsake us (Heb. 13:5). Our struggle does not go unnoticed; God is with us every moment, refining us more and more into the image of His Son.

3. **"Do you feel trapped?"** We don't have to give in to that "caged in" feeling. We can overcome our emotions of helplessness by remembering these words: "For the law of the Spirit of life in Christ Jesus has set you free from the law of sin and of death" (Rom. 8:2). God has given His Holy Spirit the task of breaking us free from the prison of sin

and death. We can keep walking back into our former cells, but the Spirit is prodding us to go out into the fresh air of freedom.

   **4. "Do you feel tired?"** We wear ourselves out trying to live for God by our own power. How foolish can we be? If we could not save ourselves, what makes us think that we can sanctify ourselves? God is the One who has saved us, and He is the One who will sanctify us through His Spirit (vv. 3–4). Our task is not to work for holiness but to cooperate with the Holy Spirit as He makes us holy.

**B. Help from the Spirit.** From what we have seen so far, the Spirit's work is obvious: *He does for us what we cannot do for ourselves, and He fulfills in us all that God desires* (v. 4). This does not negate the fact that we will walk through some dark valleys. Neither does it deny that we must actively submit to the Spirit's work by seeking to obey God's Word. However, this text does inform us that we are not alone in our battle. The Holy Spirit is actively working to make us into the people that we should be.

## IV. Some Lessons to Be Learned.

Permeating these verses of Scripture are two truths we would be wise to remember.

**A. A life without struggles is impossible.** Even after God has *declared* us righteous, His next step is to *make* us righteous. That's what sanctification is all about. But it's not easy. The process is pockmarked with difficulties, because we are still sinners.

**B. A struggle without surrender is miserable.** We can fight the Spirit's work and consequently experience defeat; or we can cooperate with Him and find acceptance, hope, freedom, and refreshment. The choice is ours; the work is His.

*Living Insights*

"For the law of the Spirit of life in Christ Jesus has set you free from the law of sin and of death" (Romans 8:2). Isn't it great to be a free spirit? Paul devotes an entire letter to the subject of freedom. Let's check it out.

- After you copy this chart into your notebook, turn to the Epistle of Galatians. As you read through the six chapters, jot down some *principles of freedom* that you observe. They will provide some great background material for you as we continue through Romans 8.

| Freedom in Christ—Galatians | |
|---|---|
| Principles of Freedom | Passages in Galatians |
| | |

 *Living Insights*

A life without struggles is impossible. A struggle without surrender is miserable. Are you experiencing this surrender in your life?

- If you've been struggling and not surrendering, now's the time to change. Make this "Living Insights" a memorable one. Turn it into a time of releasing your conflicts. Give them to God. You may want to do it quietly in your mind, audibly in words, or maybe visibly in written form. The point is *do it now.* We're human. We really do need His help. The Lord does understand. So, give those struggles to Him.

# Talking about Walking
*Romans 8:1–13*

We all want a fulfilling life—one that will allow us to reach our maximum potential in an environment relatively free from conflict and stress. But Romans 7:1–8:4 informs us that such a life is more ideal than real. Nonetheless, we still long to be less frustrated in our walk with the Lord, and we deeply desire greater balance and consistency. Can we experience this kind of life? God's answer is yes, but the outworking of His response involves drastic changes in our mental attitudes and behavioral habits. These alterations are not humanly possible. But, as we shall see, they are divinely possible and are already being made in the lives of Christians.

**I.  The Believer before God** (Romans 8:1–4).

In Romans 7 we receive an honest appraisal of the Christian life as it is worked out by human effort alone. When we live by our own power, we experience condemnation, hopelessness, entrapment, and exhaustion. The Apostle Paul found this way of life so overwhelming that he called out in anguish, "Wretched man that I am! Who will set me free from the body of this death?" (7:24). Beginning in chapter 8, we learn that there is an answer to this question. And the answer we find informs us of three facts that are true of all Christians.

**A. Eternally Secure** (v. 1). The text reads, "There is therefore now no condemnation for those who are in Christ Jesus." Believers are neither under God's wrath nor susceptible to the everlasting judgment that is the final result of His wrath. In other words, their salvation is secure forever. It makes no difference what they are experiencing in their walk with God. Even if their struggle climaxes with a cry acknowledging their wretchedness, they are no longer under divine condemnation but divine grace. We who have put our faith in Jesus Christ are saved for the rest of time and beyond. We can never lose our salvation because it does not depend on us but on God. Once we are *in* Christ by faith, it is the Lord who keeps us there forever (cf. John 10:27–30, Rom. 8:35–39).

**B. Internally Free** (v. 2). At the moment of salvation, a believer is also set free "from the law of sin and of death." The Holy Spirit enters the life of a new Christian and internally releases him from those anchors that weighed him down in sin. And, as we shall see, this same Spirit empowers a believer to grow in and enjoy his newfound liberty.

**C. Positionally Perfect** (vv. 3–4). These verses tell us that although God's Law infallibly spelled out perfect righteousness, it could not be perfectly obeyed by sinful human beings. However, what man could not do, "God did." And He

21

accomplished the task by "sending His own Son in the likeness of sinful flesh and as an offering for sin." Through Christ's death and resurrection, the Father "condemned sin in the flesh, *in order that the requirement of the Law might be fulfilled in us, who do not walk according to the flesh, but according to the Spirit*" (emphasis added). Consequently, we who trust in Christ for our salvation are given the perfect righteousness we could not otherwise obtain. Of course, this does not mean that we are now sinless. The Book of Romans teaches just the opposite (see 6:12–14, 7:14–25). But it does mean that since we are *in* God's righteous Son, we are positionally perfect. The Lord sees us through Christ and, therefore, *declares* us righteous. But He also knows that our actual condition does not yet match our theological position. That's why He exhorts us to move toward holiness in the power of the Holy Spirit. Indeed, He assumes as fact that we are already walking "according to the Spirit." We really have no choice in the matter. If we are believers, then the Holy Spirit has already begun to transform us according to the divine standard of holiness.

**II. The Contrast between Lifestyles** (Romans 8:5–11).
Before examining this passage, we need to briefly address an exegetical question. Some Bible students claim that these verses contrast two groups of Christians—spiritual and carnal. The problem with this interpretation comes in verse 9: "However, you are not in the flesh but in the Spirit, if indeed the Spirit of God dwells in you. But if anyone does not have the Spirit of Christ, he does not belong to Him." Everyone who has been saved does have the Holy Spirit dwelling in him and now orders his life according to the same Spirit. Everyone who has not been saved does not possess the indwelling ministry of the Holy Spirit and now directs his life according to the flesh. Therefore, these verses *do* contrast two different groups of people as well as two diverse lifestyles, but they do *not* contrast carnal and spiritual Christians. Rather, they expose the differences between the non-Christian's fleshly life and the Christian's spiritual life. Let's explore each one separately.

    **A. Life according to the Flesh.** There are several traits that characterize the fleshly life of an unbeliever.

        **1. A Fleshly Mind-set** (v. 5a). Non-Christians have a mental orientation toward sin. Their dominating impulses are set against God.

        **2. A Deathlike Existence** (v. 6a). An unbeliever's life is empty, futile, and plagued by guilt.

        **3. A Godward Hostility** (v. 7a). Within their mind-set, non-Christians have clenched fists raised toward heaven in open defiance of the King.

**4. A Rebellious Lifestyle** (v. 7b). Those without Christ refuse to submit themselves to God's standard of right and wrong. Instead, they go their own way ... they do their own thing.

**5. An Inability to Obey or Please God** (vv. 7b–8). Unbelievers could not submit to God on their own power even if they wanted to. The only way anyone can be saved and become righteous is by the redemptive work of Christ and the transforming work of the Holy Spirit. But since unbelievers have not accepted this way of life by faith, they could not possibly live it and thereby please God.

**B. Life according to the Spirit.** In contrast to the lifestyle of the unbeliever is that of the believer. Let's go back to verse 5 and probe into each Christian trait as it occurs.

**1. A Spiritual Mind-set** (v. 5b). The Holy Spirit creates in believers a deep-seated orientation toward righteousness. Consequently, their innermost drives are to do good rather than evil.

**2. A Vital Experience** (v. 6b). Because believers are no longer under God's wrath, they have "life and peace." Non-Christians can never experience these apart from Christ and the Holy Spirit.

**3. A Spirit-Indwelt Life** (v. 9). The transforming power of the Lord's Spirit abides in all believers, molding them into the holy people God wants them to be.

**4. Spiritually Alive** (v. 10). When individuals become Christians, they die to sin and become spiritually alive forever. Their physical bodies, however, do not receive immortality right away. The bodies of believers remain subject to physical death, even though they will be resurrected and thereby become immortal (1 Cor. 15:50–57).

**5. The Power of Resurrection Life** (v. 11). Although Christians' bodies will be raised from the dead in the future, this verse says that they have spiritual resurrection life in the present. While their bodies decay, inwardly they are being renewed into the everlasting image of Christ (2 Cor. 4:16, Col. 3:10–11).

**III. The Obligations before Us** (Romans 8:12–13).

According to Paul's instruction, we who have the Spirit of God are responsible for two actions.

**A. Do not live fleshly** (vv. 12–13a). In this text, a negative command is given: "So then, brethren, we are under obligation, not to the flesh, to live according to the flesh—for if you are living according to the flesh, you must die." We are obligated by the Lord to stop engaging in a sinful lifestyle. And since He has given us His Spirit, we now have the supernatural ability needed to obey this command.

**B. Do live spiritually** (v. 13b). On the positive side, we are responsible to allow the Holy Spirit to put "to death the deeds of the body." We cannot mature in the Christian faith without placing ourselves at God's disposal. We must rely upon Him to make us righteous. Paul tells us how we can do this in the following passage: "I urge you therefore, brethren, by the mercies of God, to present your bodies a living and holy sacrifice, acceptable to God, which is your spiritual service of worship" (Rom. 12:1).

## IV. Some Questions We Must Ask.

This is a great section of Scripture. Now that we have taken some time to understand it, let's take some equally valuable moments to appropriate it. For your benefit, let's personalize these applications.

**A. Are you absolutely sure that you're a Christian?** If so, then continue to rest confidently in the fact of your salvation. If you are unsure about your salvation, then settle it today. Accept by faith Jesus' death on the cross for your sins, then be assured that you are secure in Him forever.

**B. Is your mind set on the flesh or on the Spirit?** If your mind is oriented toward a life of sin, then you need Christ as your Savior. If your mind is geared toward a life of godliness, then commit yourself wholeheartedly to the Spirit's work in your life.

*Living Insights*

**Study One** ▬▬▬▬▬▬▬▬▬▬▬▬▬▬▬▬▬▬▬▬▬▬▬▬▬▬▬▬▬▬▬▬▬▬▬▬▬▬▬▬

Unquestionably, one of the great chapters of the Bible is Romans 8. There are many significant concepts in this passage that are worthy of more study. Let's take time for that right now.

● Make a copy of the following chart in your notebook. Carefully read Romans 8 and write down all the words you consider to be key to understanding the text. Start with verses 1–11. Then go further if you have more time. Seek to determine the meaning of each word from the text itself. If you encounter a difficult section, check other passages of Scripture and a good Bible dictionary. Finally, write down a sentence explaining why each word you chose is important to the chapter.

| Talking about Walking—Romans 8 | | | |
|---|---|---|---|
| Key Words | Verses | Definitions | Significance |
| | | | |

 *Living Insights*

**Study Two** ▬▬▬▬▬▬▬▬▬▬▬▬▬▬▬▬▬▬▬▬▬▬▬▬▬▬▬▬▬▬▬▬▬▬▬▬▬▬▬▬

Let's think through Romans 8 on a personal level. Use the following ideas to help stimulate your thinking in this personalization process. Be honest in your answers.

● Eternally secure, internally free, and positionally perfect . . . which one encourages you the most? Can you explain why?

● In verses 5–8, what are the characteristics of a fleshlike existence? Do any of those traits plague your life? If so, which ones?

● Describe the progression of thought in verses 9–11. What difference does the indwelling ministry of the Holy Spirit make in the lives of Christians? Why is it important for the Spirit to give life to our bodies? Could you live a godly life without the Holy Spirit within you?

# A Spirit-Controlled Mind-set
*Romans 8:12–17*

Through our study of Romans, we are coming to realize that many of us have been taught incorrectly. Instead of being instructed to claim the divine power we possess and to live above the drag of our sinful nature, we are merely told what to do *after* we sin. Our mind-set has been nurtured by corrective theology rather than preventive theology. Thus, we have come to *expect* failure, disobedience, and resistance in our lives, and we have learned to *focus* our attention on sin instead of on righteousness. It's no wonder that this kind of teaching has led many of us to both a defeatist attitude and a view of life as one of endurance rather than enjoyment. The good news is that God did not save us so that we could suffer through a miserable existence. His plan is that we live on a much higher plane. In the section of Romans we are about to delve into, Paul provides us with a whole new perspective on the Christian life. Let's be open to his liberating message.

## I. An Initial Question.

Paul has made it very clear that salvation is a gift made available to us by God's grace. Since we were dead in our sin, separated from God and under His wrath, we were completely unable to earn His acceptance. Our only hope of being spared from everlasting judgment was found in the merciful action of God. Thankfully, He chose to deliver us by sending His Son to die in our behalf. Because Christ willingly paid the penalty for our sin, we have an avenue of escape from death and a divine promise of everlasting life. Thus, those of us who have exercised faith in Christ's redemptive work have been saved by the Lord. He alone has rescued us and made us forever secure in His Son. But *who makes us holy?* Is God responsible for our sanctification or are we?

## II. The Biblical Answer.

Many Christians have taught, at least by implication, that we are to strive for our own sanctification: the Lord has saved us, now it's our task to become godly people. This is *not* what Scripture teaches. The biblical view is that *sanctification, like salvation, is a work of God.* We are called to cooperate with Him through the process. We are never told to perform the job ourselves. Let's briefly examine some texts that affirm this truth.

    **A. Philippians 1:6.** In this passage we read that "He who began a good work in you will perfect it until the day of Christ Jesus." The Lord not only rescued us from the penalty of sin, but He also rescues us from the power of sin. In fact, He promises to daily promote our development toward holiness until Christ returns for us in glory. At that wonderful moment, God will make us perfectly righteous in actuality, not just in position.

**B. Ephesians 2:8–10.** These verses explain that God saved us by His grace through our faith alone. They go on to say that "we are His workmanship, created in Christ Jesus for good works, which God prepared beforehand, that we should walk in them." From the moment of our conversion to Christ, the Lord began to change us. And like a potter working a clump of clay, it is God who designs, molds, and develops us into the flawless vessels He desires. All He requires from us is that we cooperate with Him through the vessel-making process.

**C. First Thessalonians 5:23–24.** This text makes the point even more explicit: "Now may the God of peace Himself sanctify you entirely; and may your spirit and soul and body be preserved complete, without blame at the coming of our Lord Jesus Christ. Faithful is He who calls you, and He also will bring it to pass." There is no hint here that the sanctification task is ours to perform. Indeed, how could sinners, even saved ones, ever purify themselves? The Lord is both our Savior and Sanctifier. He will make us completely faultless . . . entirely sinless . . . perfectly holy at the moment of Christ's return.

## III. Our Personal Obligations.

We have discovered that the sanctification process is not only God's handiwork, but it also requires our cooperation. So the question is, How can we get in line with the Lord's program? Asked another way, What can we do to facilitate rather than hamper God's work in us? In Romans 8:12–13, the Apostle Paul informs us that there are two actions we can take. Both of them are *obligations*—we are morally, spiritually, and legally bound by God to make these choices.

**A. Not to the Flesh** (vv. 12–13a). We are told in this passage that we are not to bind ourselves to "the flesh." In other words, we are no longer obligated to engage in a sinful lifestyle. But through Jesus Christ, we have been set free. This text also informs us that a life characterized by the flesh leads to death. Whenever we return to a rebellious manner of living, we begin to experience the misery of a deathlike existence. Inner turmoil and agony, hostility, resentment, irritability, and selfishness are all hallmarks of this way of life. And if the Holy Spirit fails to get our attention through these means, then He uses other avenues, such as financial loss, illness, unemployment, and intense personal struggle. If we insist on living in sin, the Lord can even end our physical lives (1 Cor. 11:27–32). The fact that God disciplines us shows that He takes our sanctification seriously.

**B. But to the Spirit** (v. 13b). In contrast to the lifestyle of the flesh is the lifestyle of the Spirit. As born-again children of God, we are obligated to commit ourselves to the transforming work of the Holy Spirit. When we place ourselves in His hands and draw upon His power, we will be enabled to die daily to sin. Then, and only then, will we begin to experience real living. In short, *the key to the Christian life is personal commitment to and cooperation with the Spirit's work in our lives.*

## IV. Some Internal Manifestations.

What can we expect when we quit trying to control our lives and willingly give God free reign? What occurs when the Spirit-controlled mind-set begins to operate? Romans 8:14–17 reveals four manifestations of the Spirit's work that we can anticipate.

A. **Practical, Everyday Leading from God** (v. 14). The Greek term for *led* in this verse means "to show the way, to guide." We are daily guided by the Spirit of God as we make ourselves available to Him. We can rest assured that He will never lead us to contradict the Scriptures, but He will always show us opportunities to flesh out biblical truth in life.

B. **Fearless Intimacy with God** (v. 15). This verse states "For you have not received a spirit of slavery leading to fear again, but you have received a spirit of adoption as sons by which we cry out, 'Abba! Father!' " God has not only saved us from sin, but He has adopted us into His forever family. As a consequence, we now enjoy intimacy with the Lord. Our relationship with Him is so close and unrestrictive that we can approach Him as a Palestinian child did his father. We can address Him as *Abba,* which is Aramaic for "Daddy."

C. **Assurance of Belonging to God** (v. 16). Another manifestation of the Spirit's controlling work in our lives is that the "Spirit Himself bears witness with our spirit that we are children of God." He reassures us and testifies with us that our salvation in Christ is secure.

D. **Reminder of Value and Worth before God** (v. 17). We who are believers are "heirs of God and fellow heirs with Christ, if indeed we suffer with Him in order that we may also be glorified with Him." The glory that is Christ's by right will be inherited by us through grace (John 17:22–24). However, there is a necessary prelude to glory, and that is suffering (cf. 1 Pet. 4:13, 5:10). The afflictions and privations that destroy us externally are the means God's Spirit uses to transform us internally. This internal change reaches its goal when our physical bodies die and our spiritual condition becomes conformed perfectly to Christ's image (cf. 2 Cor. 4:7–11, 16–17). What a profound demonstration of our value and worth in God's sight!

## V. Some Personal Application.

As we reflect on what we have learned in this lesson, there are two primary questions we need to answer.

  **A. Who is in control of your life?** Are you severing yourself from sin by yielding to the Spirit's control? Or do you still find yourself submitting to your old master? If you have accepted Christ's redemptive work by faith, then the Holy Spirit has already begun to change you from the inside out. Don't thwart His work. Commit yourself daily to cooperate with His perfect design for your life.

  **B. What gives your life significance?** Is it your home, family, spouse, friends, money, possessions, job, hobbies, or ministry? Or is your sense of value and worth derived from what God has done, is doing, and will do in your life? Your answer will reveal where your ultimate commitment and priorities lie.

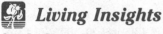 *Living Insights*

One of the key observations that can be made after reading Romans 8 is the *contrast* between the flesh and the Spirit. In order to highlight the differences between these two lifestyles, let's chart our way through this chapter.

● Read through Romans 8:1–17 one more time. After you've copied the chart below, write down each statement made about the flesh and the Spirit. Wrap it all up by making some conclusions based on your study.

| The Contrasts—Romans 8:1–17 | |
|---|---|
| Flesh | Spirit |
| | |
| Conclusions | |
| | |

*Living Insights*

In Romans 8:14–17, we found four internal manifestations of the Spirit-controlled mind-set. Let's spend some time reflecting on what these manifestations mean. Jot down *why* each one is beneficial to you and *how* you've seen it demonstrated in your life. Conclude by thanking the One *who* made it possible for you to enjoy these rich rewards.

- Practical, Everyday Leading from God
- Fearless Intimacy with God
- Assurance of Belonging to God
- Reminder of Our Value and Worth before God

# The Glory and the Groan
*Romans 8:16–27*

The first part of Romans 8 has concentrated on the believer's intimate relationship with Christ. We are forever secure in Him (v. 1). Because of His death and resurrection, we have been liberated from the dominating authority of sin and death (vv. 2–4). Through the indwelling power of His Holy Spirit, we are becoming righteous (v. 10). We are also led daily by His Spirit (v. 14); we have been adopted as sons into His forever family (v. 15); and we have become fellow heirs of His magnificent glory (v. 17). All of these tremendous truths *could* imply that we will never experience difficulties, but the opposite is indeed true. Among the numerous questions this fact may raise, the Apostle Paul basically deals with two in verses 16–27: What perspective should we have on our sufferings? And what help does God give us for persevering through them? The answers found in this passage can provide comfort and courage to any believer who suffers, no matter how intensely.

## I. The Presence of Suffering.

In a subtle manner, Paul introduces the subject of suffering and how it relates to the Christian life.

### A. Certainty and Purpose Declared (vv. 16–17).

Paul tells us that the Holy Spirit proclaims with our spirit that we are truly saved. To this he adds that we are "heirs of God and fellow heirs with Christ." In other words, the glory that belongs to Christ will one day be ours as well. After conveying this wonderful truth about the future, Paul relates another fact that jerks us back to the present: "If indeed we suffer with Him in order that we may also be glorified with Him." The Greek terms translated *if indeed* do not convey the idea of "perhaps" or "maybe." This grammatical construction communicates absolute certainty. A good rendering of it would be "for sure." Paul is telling us that we *will* suffer; there is no doubt about it. Indeed, we will suffer "with Him." That is, we will share in Christ's sufferings by experiencing affliction and struggle in our own lives. For some of us, sharing in Christ's sufferings will involve a painful, debilitating disease. Others of us will experience the ache of a broken home, or the unexpected loss of a loved one. Whatever the manner or means, the ultimate goal of suffering is the joy of glorification. The Lord uses our trials and tribulations to purge us of sin, to bring us closer to Himself, and to conform us more completely to the image of His Son (cf. 2 Cor. 4:7–11, 16–17; Heb. 12:1–13, James 1:2–4, 1 Pet. 4:12–19). At this time, we do not fully understand how our suffering is bringing about this renewal, but we can rest assured that it will accomplish its God-ordained purpose (1 John 3:2).

32

**B. Present and Future Compared** (v. 18). In this passage we are assured that "the sufferings of this present time are not worthy to be compared with the glory that is to be revealed to us." There is no comparison between our present afflictions and our future glory. In fact, when we are ushered into Christ's presence, we will bathe in the everlasting joy that far exceeds the temporary groans now threatening to drown us.

**C. Analogy and Principles Shared** (vv. 19–22). Concerning our present pain and future glory, Paul draws an analogy from creation itself. He tells us that "the anxious longing of the creation waits eagerly for the revealing of the sons of God" (v. 19). When all believers are finally glorified—fully transformed in body and soul to the image of Christ—the universe will be recreated to a state at least equal to its condition before the Fall of man (Rev. 21–22). The whole created order waits expectantly for this glorious event. From this magnificent picture of the future, we can gain a proper perspective on our present sufferings. Verses 19–22 help us toward this end by revealing four principles.

1. **Groaning is temporary** (v. 19). When we look around, we see numerous indications that the world is decaying and dying. But the Scriptures proclaim that creation's groans will not last forever. They will come to an end when believers inherit Christ, the radiant glory of God.

2. **Groaning is a consequence** (v. 20a). The creation did not ask to be "subjected to futility." Rather, it was an act of God in response to man's sin. When the universe was first brought into existence, the Lord declared it to be "very good" (Gen. 1:31). The earth itself was a paradise filled with luscious plants and trees that yielded beautiful flowers and delicious fruits (Gen. 1:29–30, 2:8–14). However, one of the consequences of Adam's sin was the cursing of the ground (Gen. 3:17–18). God caused the earth to become a victim of corruption because of man's disobedience.

3. **Groaning is a means to an end** (vv. 20b–21). The world was placed under the curse of sin "in hope that the creation itself also [would] be set free from its slavery to corruption into the freedom of the glory of the children of God." The enslavement and corruption the world now experiences will end after Christians are glorified and non-Christians are judged. Following these events, the Lord will create "a new heaven and a new earth" (Rev. 21:1). In this new world of ineffable beauty, there will be no tears, death, mourning, pain, and night (Rev. 21:4, 22:5). The glory of God will

illumine the earth, and the Lamb of God will be its lamp (21:23, 22:5). The curse imposed because of sin will be lifted from the whole created order. Thus, the present groans serve as a means to future glory.

4. **Groaning is universal** (v. 22). This verse in Romans states that "the whole creation groans and suffers the pains of childbirth together until now." Nothing in the universe is exempt from the effects of sin. And the consequences experienced by the world are like the intense pain felt by a woman in labor. But just as the pain of labor is quickly forgotten after the birth of each child, so the groans of creation will fade from memory once we are ushered into glory.

## II. The Response of the Sufferer.

Now Paul turns from the general suffering of creation to the particular suffering of creatures—in this case, believers. He points out that our response to the present situation is similar to that of the rest of creation.

A. **Groaning and Longing** (v. 23). Not only does the world groan under the corruption caused by sin, "but also we ourselves, having the first fruits of the Spirit, even we ourselves groan within ourselves, waiting eagerly for our adoption as sons, the redemption of our body." Deep within us resides a taste of the wonderful inheritance that will one day be ours. When we finally receive it in full, our bodies will emerge immortally whole and perfect. No blindness, paralysis, disease, age, or any other detrimental parasite will mark them. They will be free from all defects and faults forever.

B. **Hoping and Waiting** (vv. 24–25). These verses tell us that full salvation is ours now, but all of its benefits will not be received until later. So "with perseverance we wait eagerly" to inherit the many riches that are ours in Christ Jesus.

C. **Praying and Searching** (vv. 26–27). As we struggle through our groans, we can rest assured that "the Spirit . . . helps our weakness." Even when "we do not know how to pray as we should, . . . the Spirit Himself intercedes for us with groanings too deep for words; and He who searches the hearts knows what the mind of the Spirit is, because He intercedes for the saints according to the will of God." The Lord never abandons us, regardless of the intensity of our struggle. Our Heavenly Father has even provided the Holy Spirit to pray for us so that His perfect will might be worked out in our lives.

## III. For Those of Us Who Suffer.

From what we have learned, there are two conclusions to be drawn that will provide comfort and strength through even the darkest valleys.

**A. The greater the groan the greater the glory.**
**B. The weaker our spirit the stronger His support.**

 *Living Insights*

Romans 8:18 speaks of "the glory that is to be revealed." What a promise! Let's do some digging in order to discover what that glory includes.

- With the assistance of a good Bible concordance, let's do a study on the word *glory*. Make a copy of this chart and in the left column begin recording each verse that contains the word *glory*. In the other column, write a statement of clarification explaining how *glory* is used in each verse.

| A Word Study on *Glory* | |
| --- | --- |
| References | Clarification |
| | |

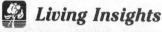 *Living Insights*

Don't forget—the greater the groan the greater the glory. Let's concentrate our efforts on experiencing the "foretaste of glory" spoken of in Fanny Crosby's great hymn titled "Blessed Assurance, Jesus Is Mine."

- One of the finest ways to experience God's glory is through the vehicle of *music*. How about using your "Living Insights" time to sing praises to God? Give thanks to Him by singing psalms, hymns, and spiritual songs (Col. 3:16). Don't hurry through the lyrics; instead, meditate on them. Here are a few suggested titles to get you started:
    —"Blessed Assurance, Jesus Is Mine"
    —"Leaning on the Everlasting Arms"
    —"All Hail the Power of Jesus' Name"
    —"A Mighty Fortress Is Our God"
    —"Under His Wings"

# Providence Made Practical
*Romans 8:26–30*

Following a passage in which suffering and groaning are hallmarks, the Apostle Paul now provides believers with encouragement and hope. He does not leave us locked into the horizontal outlook of man, but he does bring relief by giving us the vertical perspective of God. The first ray of hope comes when he tells us that the Holy Spirit intercedes on our behalf "according to the will of God" (vv. 26–27). What an uplifting thought! But there is still more to be grasped. We need to understand that the Spirit's intercessory support works effectively for both our good and God's glory. Fortunately, Paul gives us this information and helps us to see a second ray of hope in divine providence.

## I. Wrestling with God's Providence.

The pain we feel because of our groanings can be alleviated by a knowledge of the providence of God. The Bible clearly teaches that all happenings are under divine control (see Pss. 33:6–11, 103:19; Isa. 14:24–27; Matt. 6:25–34; Eph. 1:11). Sometimes we find solace in that truth. Often, however, we tend to wrestle with divine providence and its consequences. In Romans 8, Paul suggests three reasons for our struggle and two facts we tend to forget when we consider God's sovereignty.

### A. Three Reasons We Wrestle.
The first one is embedded in these words: "The mind set on the flesh is hostile toward God; for it does not subject itself to the law of God, for it is not even able to do so" (Rom. 8:7). In other words, *in the flesh we are selfish*. We want our way, not anyone else's—especially not God's. We are set against Him and His plan for our lives. A second reason we struggle is that *in the flesh we are afraid*. We fear losing control over our lives and becoming subject to a plan that is of His design. We do not mind reaping the everlasting benefits of God's sovereign control (vv. 23–25), but we often lack the courage to face the groans that must precede those glorious benefits. The third reason for our wrestling with God's providence is that *in the flesh we are proud*. The Lord knows we are weak and totally dependent on Him (vv. 26–27; cf. John 15:5), but we have difficulty admitting this to ourselves and others.

### B. Two Facts We Forget.
Thinking about God's control over our lives and finding ourselves tempted to question it, we often fail to recall two essential truths. One is that *our focus is on the immediate, while God's is on the ultimate*. We tend to view our lives as complex puzzles with a multitude of pieces. As we try to put our lives together, we can become frustrated and

37

confused. The reason for this is that we seldom see how the varied pieces fit together. In fact, since we are limited in our knowledge and perspective, we do not even know what the puzzle picture of our lives will finally look like. God, on the other hand, infallibly sees the completed picture of each individual. So what may seem out of place and uncalled for to us is not so from the Lord's perspective. The second fact we tend to forget is that *our knowledge is limited, while God's is unlimited.* After a good deal of research and reflection, we can gain a fair understanding of the past and the present. Our knowledge, however, will always be subject to growth and correction. This is not so with God; His knowledge is complete and perfect. He not only knows every detail of the past and present with total accuracy, but He also knows everything about the future. Nothing can take Him by surprise, for "all things are open and laid bare to the eyes of Him with whom we have to do" (Heb. 4:13b).

## II. Thinking through God's Providence.

As we begin to probe further into the subject of divine providence, we must understand that we cannot fully comprehend it. The only way we could ever have a complete grasp on God's will is if we were infinite as He is. But that is impossible. Creatures who are limited by nature could never become unlimited. Therefore, we must be content with a partial understanding of this infinitely vast topic. Fortunately, the Lord has revealed through Paul's words in Romans 8:28–30 some truths we can confidently embrace concerning His sovereignty. These vital facts are divided between an unconditional promise and an unfathomable basis. Let's examine them under their respective categories.

   **A. The Promise** (v. 28). Read the words of this verse slowly and reflectively: "And we know that God causes all things to work together for good to those who love God, to those who are called according to His purpose." As we consider these words, we can readily see that they convey four prominent thoughts.

   1. **The promise is to be claimed, not ignored.** The Greek term for *know* in this context refers to the possession of absolute, unshakable confidence. The promise is not something we wish for or guess at, but it is a truth in which we can have total assurance because it's given by the Lord. Therefore, we should embrace it and make it a vital part of our daily lives.

   2. **The project is God's, not ours.** The passage says that "God causes all things to work together." Please observe that it does *not* say, "God causes all things to occur." We know from other biblical texts that the Lord is not the cause of sin and evil (Hab. 1:13; James 1:13; 1 John 1:5, 2:16).

Scripture also clearly states that God is not the only cause of good motives or actions, but people are as well (Ex. 1:15–21; Josh. 2:1–14; Matt. 7:9–11; Luke 7:36–50, 10:38–42). So what does Romans 8:28 teach? It informs us that the Lord uses everything that enters our lives to work together for our best interest. He is the master Potter and we are His clay. He uses whatever means are necessary to form us into vessels of the utmost grace and beauty. Furthermore, as the Potter, He has every right to design and shape us into whatever He desires (Jer. 18:1–11). But we can rest assured in the fact that because He is all-good, He will always do what is best for us.

3. **The plan is total, not partial.** The Lord causes *"all things to work together for good"* (emphasis added). Many times we do not see, even in retrospect, how some events in our lives could possibly be for our good. But simply because we may be unable to figure out all the whys and the hows does not imply that God is without good reason or that He has lost control. After all, He sees everything clearly and knows all things completely. We, on the other hand, "see in a mirror dimly" and only "know in part" (1 Cor. 13:12). So it only stands to reason that we who do not even fully know ourselves will not always understand the all-good plan of the omniscient God.

4. **The purpose is good, not evil.** The Lord will not cause or permit anything to cross our paths that will be to our detriment. Every circumstance is designed for our ultimate good. The Lord is for us, not against us. Too many times we live as if the opposite were true. And when we do, we miss some of the richest benefits that God is waiting to give us.

**B. The Basis** (vv. 29–30). Among the many truths conveyed in these verses, two are prominent. First, the foundational *model* for God's sovereign activity in the lives of believers is Jesus Christ. God has predestined them "to become conformed to the image of His Son" (v. 29). In other words, the Heavenly Father wants to reproduce in us the character qualities of Christ. Even before He created us, He was committed to this task; and He will not quit until He finishes it in every Christian. Second, the foundational *process* by which He brings about this Christlikeness in believers is spelled out in a five-link chain: "For whom He *foreknew,* He also *predestined* . . . ; and whom He predestined, these He also *called;* and whom He called, these He also *justified;* and whom He justified, these He also *glorified"* (emphasis added). Because God can see the beginning and the end, He can speak of our perfect conformity to Christ's image as if it has already been completed. Indeed, since the entire project is His, we can be certain that the Lord will finish the work He has begun in our lives.

## III. Responding to God's Providence.

There are three stages of response Christians often pass through when they come face to face with the biblical teaching on God's providence.

**A. Initially, there is rejection.** Our selfishness, fear, and pride help to keep us from embracing the truth of God's sovereignty. But this reaction works toward our detriment, not our benefit.

**B. Progressively, there comes toleration.** As we mature in our faith, our concept of God enlarges and our experience of His providence confirms His goodness.

**C. Ultimately, there comes realization.** We finally rest in God's perfect plan for our lives and cooperate with Him as He brings about its perfect result—complete conformity to the character of Christ. What will *your* response be today?

*Living Insights*

Since the next lesson is devoted to illustrating Romans 8:28, let's spend some time here zeroing in on the two verses that follow it.

● Romans 8:29–30 has been called the golden chain that ties together the acts of God. With the help of the following chart, do some further study on the important links that form this chain. Use a Bible dictionary or commentary to assist you in defining these doctrinal terms.

| Providence Made Practical—Romans 8:29–30 | | |
|---|---|---|
| Terms | Meanings of the Words | Personal Notes |
| *Foreknew* | | |
| *Predestined* | | |
| *Called* | | |
| *Justified* | | |
| *Glorified* | | |

41

There's a good deal of meat to chew on in this brief passage. Perhaps the best way to approach it would be by starting with the bite-sized portions that follow. Work through each suggestion carefully.

- Since Romans 8:28 begins with the conjunction *and,* we know that each verse is linked with something that appears before it. Read Romans 8:26–28 slowly. In your own words, explain the tie-in between each verse. Pay special attention to the phrase "will of God" (v. 27). What is the "will" of God for each believer? Read Romans 12:1–2 for further insight.

- Read Romans 8:28 aloud, emphasizing the words *God . . . all . . . good . . . His purpose.* What means the most to you, and what do you find particularly disturbing? Explain your answers. Do you really find that you live as if you believe this verse of Scripture? If you're struggling with it, spend some time in prayer. Ask for insight from God.

- Focus your attention on "His purpose" in verse 28. Now read the first half of verse 29. Do you see any relationship between the two? Think about the whole concept of being conformed to the image of Christ. What types of things are usually involved in this process? Why is it occasionally so painful? After you have reflected on this, share a particular example from your past—one where God worked in your life to carry out "His purpose" *against* your will.

- Locate the numerous references to God and Christ in Romans 8:28–30. You will find many of them in pronoun form. Share with someone else a particular technique you might use from day to day that could remind you of God's presence, even when those nagging interruptions come. Talk about a struggle or two that hinders you from focusing on Him through the day.

# Providence Made Personal

*Genesis 37, 45, 50*

It's important to consider a biblical doctrine from an intellectual standpoint. We must have a clear understanding of a truth before we can accurately apply it to our lives. However, many of us will not attempt to appropriate a truth until we realize that it affects us personally. When we can see that a particular doctrine is relevant to us and our situation, then we will usually take steps to flesh it out in our lives. That's what we want to do with the biblical teaching on divine providence. Our plan is to examine some snapshots from the life of an ancient believer named Joseph. By doing this, we will see that God's sovereign dealings with him are also pertinent to us. We will glean an enriching and personal picture of the words in Romans 8: "And we know that God causes all things to work together for good to those who love God, to those who are called according to His purpose" (v. 28).

## I. The Story of Joseph.

There are many scenes in Joseph's life that we could probe into and learn from, but the ones that we are most concerned with here occur in Genesis 37, 45, and 50. Let's consider each chapter consecutively and remain open to what God wants to teach us.

**A. A Beloved Son and Hated Brother** (Gen. 37). Several hundred years before Moses led the Hebrew people out of Egypt, there lived a young man named Joseph. He made his home in the land of Canaan with his father Jacob, who was also called Israel, and his many brothers. Joseph was the youngest in the family. Apparently, he was born when Jacob was old enough to be his grandfather. This caused Jacob to love him more than he loved Joseph's brothers. As a result, Jacob's other sons despised him (vv. 1–4). Eventually, their hatred was expressed through a plot to get rid of Joseph. They dug a pit, captured him, and threw him into it. Soon a caravan of Ishmaelites bound for Egypt passed their way. The brothers counseled together and decided to sell Joseph to the Ishmaelites. Then they covered up the scheme from their father by making it look like a wild beast had killed Joseph. Jacob believed the false report of his sons and grieved over Joseph, his beloved son (vv. 18–35). Meanwhile, Joseph was taken to Egypt and sold to "Potiphar, Pharaoh's officer, the captain of the bodyguard" (v. 36).

**B. An Unexpected Family Reunion** (Gen. 45). Although his brothers forgot about him, and his father buried him in his mind, Joseph was not abandoned by God. During a twelve- to fifteen-year period, he was maligned, misjudged, imprisoned, and betrayed. But the Lord saw Joseph through and used those

43

experiences to build character and strength into him. Eventually, he was made the prime minister of Egypt and put in charge of the famine relief program for all the people who lived in Egypt and Canaan. Because of his foresight and administrative skills, he was able to keep multitudes from starving to death. Of course, neither Jacob nor his sons knew that it was Joseph who was accomplishing this feat of grace. And, like everyone else, Jacob's family had to come to the Egyptian prime minister to procure the goods they would need to live. Joseph's brothers met with him a number of times without recognizing him. Finally, Joseph could stand it no longer. He sent away everyone except his brothers, and then revealed to them his identity. Needless to say, they were surprised and dismayed to learn that he was the brother they had sold into slavery (vv. 1–4). Joseph had every reason and all the power he needed to avenge himself of the wrong his brothers had done to him. But, as we can discern from his words, Joseph's perspective would not allow for revenge. Let's observe what he said to his brothers:

"I am your brother Joseph, whom you sold into Egypt. And now do not be grieved or angry with yourselves, because you sold me here; for God sent me before you to preserve life. For the famine has been in the land these two years, and there are still five years in which there will be neither plowing nor harvesting. And God sent me before you to preserve for you a remnant in the earth, and to keep you alive by a great deliverance. Now, therefore, it was not you who sent me here, but God; and He has made me a father to Pharaoh and lord of all his household and ruler over all the land of Egypt. Hurry and go up to my father, and say to him, 'Thus says your son Joseph, "God has made me lord of all Egypt; come down to me, do not delay" ' " (vv. 4b–9).

Joseph never denied that his brothers were responsible for selling him into slavery. But he did see that God used their sin to get him to Egypt so that many could be saved. And unlike his brothers, Joseph did not turn against them, but provided for a wonderful family reunion of great abundance in the land of Egypt (vv. 10–28).

C. **Death and Forgiveness** (Gen. 50). Soon after seeing Joseph again, Jacob died. Joseph and his brothers buried him in Canaan as he had requested (vv. 1–14). After they had returned to Egypt, Joseph's brothers began to fear that Joseph was holding a grudge and would pay them back in full for their wrongdoing (v. 15).

So they sent a message to Joseph, saying, "Your father charged before he died, saying, 'Thus you shall say to Joseph, "Please forgive, I beg you, the transgression of your brothers and their sin, for they did you wrong."' And now, please forgive the transgression of the servants of the God of your father" (vv. 16–17). When Joseph heard the message, he wept (v. 17b). After his brothers came humbly before him, Joseph said to them:

"Do not be afraid, for am I in God's place? And as for you, you meant evil against me, but God meant it for good in order to bring about this present result, to preserve many people alive. So therefore, do not be afraid; I will provide for you and your little ones." So he comforted them and spoke kindly to them (vv. 19–21).

Joseph was realistic. He knew that his brothers had treated him unjustly; he had not forgotten that fact. However, he also had come to realize that God had sovereignly used that free act of sin to bring about a great good. Because he had come to see even the most tragic events from the Lord's perspective, he had not become bitter. Indeed, he had become capable of exercising profound forgiveness toward his brothers who had tried to get rid of him forever.

## II. The Rest of the Story.

We are the rest of the story. We can walk away from the example of Joseph without letting it alter a single thing in our lives. Or, we can replace Joseph's name with our own and see that God's providence is personal. He is working through the events in our lives just like He did through those in Joseph's life. We may not always see His intimate involvement. But even when we are mistreated, misunderstood, suffering, or hurt in any way, we can be confident that He is causing it all "to work together for good to those who love God, to those who are called according to His purpose" (Rom. 8:28).

*Living Insights*

**Study One** ▬▬▬▬▬▬▬▬▬▬▬▬▬▬▬▬▬▬▬▬▬▬▬▬▬▬▬▬▬▬▬▬▬▬▬▬

Isn't it remarkable how the Word of God continually reinforces its own message! We can see that the truth of Romans 8:28 is demonstrated through both the Old and New Testaments.

● This lesson shows how Joseph illustrates the truth of Romans 8:28. You can either read further about the life of Joseph, or you can study some other good examples of Romans 8:28 that are listed below. As you read, make notes of how the characters handled these incidents.

—Noah (Genesis 6–8)
—Abraham (Genesis 15–22)
—Joseph (Genesis 37–50)
—Moses (Exodus 13–14)
—David (1 Samuel 18–24)
—Job (Job 1–42)
—Hosea (Hosea 1–14)
—Peter (Acts 3–5)
—Paul (Acts 27–28)

 *Living Insights*

**Study Two** ▬▬▬▬▬▬▬▬▬▬▬▬▬▬▬▬▬▬▬▬▬▬▬▬▬▬▬▬▬▬▬▬▬▬▬▬

The main purpose of this study is to make God's providence personal. What does Romans 8:28 mean in *your* life?

● Take a fresh sheet of paper, and get those creative juices flowing! Write down illustrations of Romans 8:28 from your life. Talk about both the groans and the glory. Share how you've come to the place where you can now see the good that God has brought out of evil. The examples you give might be from the past or the present, but we all have had several experiences that illustrate God's providence in our lives.

# We Overwhelmingly Conquer
*Romans 8:31–39*

The most dangerous heresy in the world today undergirds many non-Christian religions and philosophies. What is it? It is the humanistic mentality that promotes human effort and achievement as the means to gaining God's attention and favor. This brand of humanism threatens to destroy us—the sheep of God. But Romans 8:36–37 says that sheep are the overwhelming conquerors of all forms of opposition. In fact, the victory has already been secured for those who have accepted Christ as their Savior. This is a magnificent message from which we all can derive hope, courage, and solace no matter what we experience.

## I. Who helps whom?
Humanism says, "God helps those who help themselves." Christianity says, "God helps those who turn to Him for help." Scripture clearly teaches that the Creator and Sustainer of the universe does not need human effort, but that human beings desperately need Him (Acts 17:25, 30–31; Rom. 3:9–26). God helps us; we do not help Him. Let's briefly look at two of the areas in which this truth can be verified.

   **A. Salvation.** Humanism maintains that we can either win God's favor by our own efforts, or save ourselves without acknowledging God at all. Christianity, however, informs us that the only way anyone can be saved is by God's grace through faith alone (Eph. 2:8–9, Rom. 3:27–28).

   **B. Sanctification.** Again, humanism says that once we are saved, we can make ourselves into godly people. But Christianity rebuts this claim by pointing out that we cannot sanctify ourselves any more than we can save ourselves. God alone can make us holy, and He has promised that He will do so (Rom. 8:3–11, 1 Thess. 5:23–24). The motto of the humanist is, "If I try hard enough, then I'll eventually succeed." In contrast to this, the motto of the Christian is, "When I try, I fail; when I trust in Him, He succeeds."

## II. Who supports whom?
What is true of salvation and sanctification is also true of daily and ultimate victory. If we rely on ourselves, then we are doomed to defeat. However, if we place our trust in God, then victory can be ours both now and forever. But how can we be assured that God is on our side? How do we know that He will support us no matter what? The Lord Himself answers that through Paul's words in Romans 8:31–39. Let's soak up what He has to say.

   **A. A Declaration** (v. 31). Sandwiched in this verse is the divine pronouncement that "God is for us." The word *if* that precedes this statement does not imply any doubt; it would better be rendered as *since*. The text assumes and asserts that the Lord is on the side of His people.

**B. Some Questions and Answers** (vv. 31–39). This divine declaration raises several questions. These questions are all designed to produce answers that amplify and support its truth. Let's examine them and their corresponding answers. Remember, what these verses teach is meant for us to claim and apply, not simply to study.

1. **Who shall oppose us** (vv. 31–32)? Reflecting back to the truth that God is providentially working to conform us to Christ's image, Paul asks, "What then shall we say...? If God is for us, who is against us?" The assumed answer is that no one can successfully strive against us. After all, since the Lord Himself is our support and protection, who could ever overcome us? If we could be defeated, then so could God. But that is impossible. Therefore, we could never successfully be opposed. But what other proof do we have that this is true? Paul gives it to us in the form of another question: "He who did not spare His own Son, but delivered Him up for us all, how will He not also with Him freely give us all things?" In other words, since the Father freely made the ultimate sacrifice by sending His only Son to die in our behalf, will He not also freely give whatever else we need? The answer is obvious: Of course He will! The Lord will see us through to our glorification. No one will be able to thwart the achievement of His goal in our lives.

2. **Who shall accuse us** (v. 33)? Paul puts the second question in these words: "Who will bring a charge against God's elect?" Again, the expected answer is that no one will ever be able to make a case against a believer that will put his or her salvation in jeopardy. How do we know this is true? Because it is based on the fact that "God is the one who justifies." Those of us who have believed in Christ by faith alone have been declared righteous by the living God. And whoever He claims as His own, He will also glorify (v. 30b). Put another way, God will never turn to someone He has chosen through Christ and say, "I no longer choose to call you one of My own." Nor will He ever accept an accusation from anyone else that could lead to the loss of our salvation. We are forever secure in the almighty arms of God.

3. **Who shall condemn us** (v. 34)? In this passage we learn that not only is the eternal Judge of all on our side, but so is the eternal Attorney of all believers. Notice what Paul

says: "Who is the one who condemns? Christ Jesus is He who died, yes, rather who was raised, who is at the right hand of God, who also intercedes for us." The grace of God, as displayed through the death and resurrection of the Son, nullifies all opposition . . . silences all accusations . . . overrules all condemnation. No one can ever reverse God's choices. He has justified us, He is sanctifying us, and He will glorify us. Praise the Lord, nothing can stop Him!

4. **Who shall separate us** (vv. 35, 38–39)? Given all that has been said, Paul asks, "Who shall separate us from the love of Christ? Shall tribulation, or distress, or persecution, or famine, or nakedness, or peril, or sword?" No, no, a thousand times no! Nothing can sever a Christian's relationship with his Savior. And just so we would not miss the point, Paul pulls out all the stops in order to make it crystal clear: "For I am convinced that neither death, nor life, nor angels, nor principalities, nor things present, nor things to come, nor powers, nor height, nor depth, nor any other created thing, shall be able to separate us from the love of God, which is in Christ Jesus our Lord."

5. **Who shall defeat us** (vv. 36–37)? Although Paul does not ask this question directly, it is conveyed indirectly in these verses. Following a verse on suffering (Rom. 8:35) come these words from Psalm 44: "Just as it is written, 'For Thy sake we are being put to death all day long; we were considered as sheep to be slaughtered.' " The death spoken of here is not physical but is what might be labeled Personal. It is a daily dying to ourselves so that we might live more fruitfully in the Lord. Jesus referred to this death as self-denial and personal cross-bearing (Luke 9:23). Simply put, because we have been predestined to be conformed to Christ's image, we must daily yield ourselves to Him. Only in this way will we become more like Christ. As we submit to this kind of relationship in the power of the Spirit, "we overwhelmingly conquer through Him who loved us" (Rom. 8:37). The Holy Spirit enables us to conquer tribulation, distress, persecution, famine, nakedness, peril, and death as we totally abandon ourselves to His transforming work.

## III. Who needs whom?

From what we have learned, it is obvious that God does not need us, but that we desperately need Him. As we meditate on this fact, two thoughts become prominent.

49

**A. When we lose what we demand, we find what He desires.** In order to transform us into Christ's perfect character, God must strip us of those visions, dreams, rights, and desires that are contrary to His goal for our lives. This process is often painful, but the final result will be absolutely fabulous and totally fulfilling.

**B. When God removes something valuable, He replaces it with something invaluable.** He never leaves us empty-handed. Whatever God takes from us He replaces with valuables that have worth far above any price tag—riches such as peace, contentment, and satisfaction.

 *Living Insights*

**Study One** ▬▬▬▬▬▬▬▬▬▬▬▬▬▬▬▬▬▬▬▬▬▬▬

Whether it is review or a first-time discovery, Romans 8:31–39 has to be one of the most motivational passages in all of Scripture. We really do overwhelmingly conquer through Jesus Christ our Lord!

● How about taking a fresh look at this passage? Locate a version of the Scriptures that you are not accustomed to using. Read Romans 8:31–39 slowly, carefully, and thoughtfully. You'll be amazed at how the use of a different translation or paraphrase will shed new emphasis and meaning on this powerful section. Conclude your time in prayer by thanking God for the victorious message in this text.

 *Living Insights*

**Study Two** ▬▬▬▬▬▬▬▬▬▬▬▬▬▬▬▬▬▬▬▬▬▬▬

This passage is too good to leave on the page. We need to make these verses an asset to our spiritual gain. Let's do that right now!

● David hid the Word of God in his heart in order to help keep him from sinning. Let's do the same with Romans 8:31–39. In order to *memorize* this passage, try writing it out on an index card and reading it aloud repeatedly. Another good tip is to take the passage in manageable sections rather than attempting to digest all nine verses at once. No matter what method you use, you'll find that the memorizing process comes slowly and steadily, yet it does come!

# God, the Jew, and You Too
### Romans 9–11

This passage marks the beginning of the second major section in Romans. The first eight chapters present the doctrinal foundation of the letter. And the next three chapters deal with the nation of Israel. In Romans 9–11, we enter an area of special importance to God—the relationship of the gospel to His chosen people, the Jews. The argument presented is both daring and dogmatic, yet eminently logical. Before we delve into many of its details, we will use this lesson to stretch the whole scene before our eyes.

**I.  Where We Have Been** (Romans 1–8).

We can often better see where we are going after getting a handle on where we have been. With that in mind, let's take a little time to retrace the steps we have taken.

**A.  The Message of the Book.** The main theme of Romans is quite clear: God is righteous, and man can be also when he exercises faith in the redemptive work of God's only Son, Jesus Christ. When individuals do this, they are no longer subject to God's wrath and condemnation, but they become recipients of His grace and righteousness. The salvation they receive by faith alone includes their justification—salvation from sin's penalty, sanctification—salvation from sin's power, and glorification— salvation from sin's presence. Their salvation is complete, everlasting, and totally of the Lord. He saves us; He sanctifies us; and He glorifies us. We merely submit to His perfect will for our lives, and He does the rest. Furthermore, since God is providentially causing "all things to work together for good" in our lives (8:28), there is nothing that can separate us from His love (8:35–39).

**B.  The Reason for the Change.** From this brief overview of Romans 1–8, we can readily see that it would have been natural for Paul to have followed it immediately with chapter 12, verse 1: "I urge you therefore, brethren, by the mercies of God, to present your bodies a living and holy sacrifice, acceptable to God, which is your spiritual service of worship." But Paul did not do this. In fact, his mood changed from exhilarating joy to deep sorrow when he began to pen chapter 9. Notice his opening words: "I am telling the truth in Christ, I am not lying, my conscience bearing me witness in the Holy Spirit, that I have great sorrow and unceasing grief in my heart" (9:1–2). Why is there such a drastic change? The next verse gives us the answer: "For I could wish that I myself were accursed, separated from Christ for the sake of my brethren, my kinsmen according to the flesh" (v. 3). Paul's heart was breaking over the Jewish rejection of the true Messiah—Jesus of Nazareth. Why were the Jews in Paul's day turning away from Christ? From what is said in Romans 9–11, we can discern that the Jews were drawing a fallacious conclusion from these three truths: (1) the gospel is for both Jews and Gentiles; (2) the Old Testament is packed with God's promises to the Jews; and (3) only a small number of Jews have accepted the gospel. Based on these facts, many Jews arrived at this conclusion: Either the Christian understanding of the gospel is false, since so few Jews have embraced it, or God does not keep His promises. Paul knew that neither option was true. So he took three chapters to demonstrate further the validity of the Christian gospel and the absolute faithfulness of God.

## II. Where We Are Going (Romans 9–11).

Now that we have reviewed our previous steps, let's get an overview of where we are headed in Romans 9–11. By doing this, we will discover that the central message of these chapters is that *God's plan for the Jews is consistent with His character.*

   **A. Chapter 9.** The focus of this chapter is on the *sovereignty of God.* Here we peer over the divine throne in heaven and view the Jew from God's perspective. From this eternal vantage point, we learn that God's promises have not failed. The Jewish conclusion has gone awry because it assumes that everyone who is a Jew by blood relation is also a member of God's everlasting family. But, as Paul points out, "they are not all Israel who are descended from Israel; neither are they all children because they are Abraham's descendants. . . . That is, it is not the children of the flesh who are children of God, but the children of the promise are regarded as descendants" (vv. 6b–8). And how does someone become a spiritual child of God? By God's sovereign choice (vv. 9–13). Does this make the Lord unjust? "May it never be!" answers Paul (v. 14). As the master Potter, God has every right to do whatever He pleases with His "clay"—both Jews and Gentiles (vv. 15–24). Does this negate human freedom and responsibility? Not at all, for as Paul observes, the Jews who worked to obey the Law were never able to secure righteousness "because they did not pursue it by faith" (vv. 31–32). In other words, the Lord sovereignly chooses for salvation those Jews and Gentiles who trust in Christ by faith. On the other hand, He sovereignly rejects those Jews and Gentiles who try to earn their salvation. The problem is that most Jews have chosen to live by works rather than by faith. Therefore, even though God has preserved a small remnant of Jews who have accepted Christ by faith, many more are still lost in their sin.

# Insight for Living
## Cassette Tapes
### Learning to Walk by Grace

Here are sixteen biblical messages based on the central core of Paul's words to the Romans. No other section of Scripture is more important for the Christian to examine, to understand, and to apply. Romans 6–11 is actually a short course in theology, designed for the believer who is learning how to walk by grace. These doctrinal studies provide the basis for triumphant living.

---

| | U.S. | Cassette series—includes album cover ....... | $44.50 |
|---|---|---|---|
| LWG | CS | Individual cassettes—include messages A and B ............................... | 5.00 |
| | Canadian | Cassette series—includes album cover ....... | $56.50 |
| LWG | CS | Individual cassettes—include messages A and B ............................... | 6.35 |

*These prices are effective as of July 1985 and are subject to change.*

LWG 1-A: *Dying to Live*
Romans 6:1–14

    B: *Whose Slave Are You?*
Romans 6:15–23

LWG 2-A: *Portrait of a Struggling Christian*
Romans 7:1–24

    B: *Free Spirit*
Romans 7:24–8:4

LWG 3-A: *Talking about Walking*
Romans 8:1–13

    B: *A Spirit-Controlled Mind-set*
Romans 8:12–17

LWG 4-A: *The Glory and the Groan*
Romans 8:16–27

    B: *Providence Made Practical*
Romans 8:26–30

LWG 5-A: *Providence Made Personal*
Genesis 37, 45, 50

    B: *We Overwhelmingly Conquer*
Romans 8:31–39

LWG  6-A:   *God, the Jew, and You Too*
           Romans 9–11
       B:   *Straight Talk about Predestination*
           Romans 9

LWG  7-A:   *Straight Talk about Responsibility*
           Romans 10
       B:   *The Jew: Cast Off or Set Aside?*
           Romans 11:1–14

LWG  8-A:   *Horticultural Ethics*
           Romans 11:15–29
       B:   *Unsearchable, Unfathomable, Unmatched!*
           Romans 11:30–36

# Order Form

## Please send me the following cassette tapes:

The current series: ☐ LWG CS Learning to Walk by Grace

Individual tapes: ☐ LWG 1 ☐ LWG 2 ☐ LWG 3 ☐ LWG 4
☐ LWG 5 ☐ LWG 6 ☐ LWG 7 ☐ LWG 8

## I am enclosing:

$_____ To purchase cassette series for $44.50 (in Canada $56.50*) which includes the album cover

$_____ To purchase individual cassettes at $5.00 each (in Canada $6.35*)

$_____ Total of purchases

$_____ California residents please add 6% sales tax

$_____ *British Columbia residents please add 7% sales tax

$_____ Canadian residents please add 6% for postage

$_____ U.S. residents please add 10% for first-class shipping and handling if desired

$_____ Gift for the Insight for Living radio ministry for which a tax-deductible receipt will be issued

$_____ **TOTAL AMOUNT DUE (please do not send cash)**

*Form of payment:*
☐ *Check or money order made payable to Insight for Living*
☐ *Credit card (VISA or MasterCard only)*
*If there is a balance:* ☐ *Apply it as a donation* ☐ *Please refund*

---

*CREDIT CARD PURCHASES:*
☐ *VISA* ☐ *MasterCard No.* _____
*Expiration Date* _____
*Signature* _____
*We cannot process your credit card purchase without your signature.*

---

Name_____

Address_____

City _____ Radio Station_____

State/Province _____ Zip/Postal Code _____

Telephone ( ) _____
*Just in case there is a question concerning your order*

Mail your order to one of the following addresses:

*Insight for Living*
*Sales Department*
*Post Office Box 4444*
*Fullerton, CA 92634*

*Insight for Living Ministries*
*Post Office Box 2510*
*Vancouver, BC*
*Canada V6B 3W7*

# Additional Ordering Information

**Payment Options:** We accept personal checks, money orders, Visa, and MasterCard in payment for materials ordered. Unfortunately, we are unable to offer invoicing or COD orders. If the amount of your check or money order is less than the amount of your purchase, your check will be returned so that you may place your order again with the correct amount. All orders must be paid in full before shipment can be made.

**U.S. Ordering Information:** You are welcome to use our toll-free number (for orders only) between the hours of 8:30 A.M. and 4:00 P.M., Pacific Time. We can accept only Visa or MasterCard when ordering by phone. The number is (800) 772-8888. This number may be used anywhere in the continental United States excluding California, Hawaii, and Alaska. Orders from those areas are handled through our Sales Department at (714) 870-9161. We are unable to accept collect calls.

Your order will be processed promptly. We ask that you allow four to six weeks for delivery by fourth-class mail. If you wish your order to be shipped first-class, please add 10% of the total order (not including California sales tax) for shipping and handling.

**Canadian Ordering Information:** Your order will be processed promptly. We ask that you allow approximately four weeks for delivery by first-class mail to the U.S./Canadian border. All orders will be shipped from our office in Fullerton, California. For our listeners in British Columbia, a 7% sales tax must be added to the total of all tape orders (not including first-class postage). For further information, please contact our office at (604) 669-1916.

**Returned Checks:** There is a $10 charge for any returned check (regardless of the amount of your order) to cover processing and invoicing.

**Guarantee:** Our tapes are guaranteed for 90 days from the date of shipping against faulty performance or breakage due to a defect in the tape. For best results, please be sure your tape recorder is in good operating condition and is cleaned regularly.

## Quantity Discounts and Gift Certificates Are Available upon Request

**B. Chapter 10.** In this middle section, Paul turns his attention to the *justice of God.* He climbs down the heavenly ladder to earth and looks up to the divine throne. From his perspective, he sees that the gospel of God was within the reach of all (v. 8) and that it was offered impartially to all (vv. 11–13). Yet not everyone received the gospel when they heard it (vv. 16–21). Indeed, even though the Lord knew that a great number of Jews would not trust in the Messiah, He continued to offer them all the free gift of everlasting life (v. 21). Therefore, God has not treated the Jews unfairly. Rather, the Jews have been belligerent in their refusal to accept God's impartial offer of salvation.

**C. Chapter 11.** In the closing chapter of this section, the *faithfulness of God* has taken center stage. Here the divine and human perspectives come together to show that God has not failed to keep His promises. Indeed, the Lord has used the Jewish rejection of salvation by faith to bring salvation to the Gentiles. And, in so doing, He has made the Jews jealous of what the Gentiles have received (vv. 11–15). Does this mean that God will never fulfill the promises He made to believing Jews? Again, the answer is no. At a predetermined time in the future, the Lord will fulfill every detail of each promise that He has made to them (vv. 25–32). "Oh, the depth of the riches both of the wisdom and knowledge of God! How unsearchable are His judgments and unfathomable His ways!" (v. 33).

## III. Where We Are Now.

From this survey, we can glean at least two truths that will direct our steps through Paul's instruction concerning divine sovereignty and human responsibility.

**A. Our past and present are not necessarily models of our future.** Even though the Jews as God's chosen people have rejected the Messiah, there is still hope. God is not finished with them . . . and He has not completed His plan in our lives either. The Lord is renewing all believers into the image of Christ. He can begin that process in you if you will trust in Jesus as your Savior and cooperate with the Holy Spirit as your Transformer.

**B. Our outlook on life is not determined by circumstances but by focus.** We need to view our lives not simply from our earthly plane but also from God's heavenly vantage point. This will give us the perspective we need to live above our circumstances rather than under them.

## Living Insights

In this lesson we have a great opportunity to gain an overview of Romans 9–11. These chapters are important, yet admittedly difficult. They demand careful study.

- Copy the following chart into your notebook. We'll spend study one looking at Romans 9:1–10:15, and we'll use study two to get a handle on the remaining verses. As you read the text, ask *questions* about what it is saying. You should be able to come up with a lengthy list of them. Remember, no question is too simple or too complex; all questions are allowed and welcomed. After you write down your queries, use the text to find the appropriate answers. This process can strengthen your powers of *observation*.

| Romans 9:1–10:15 | |
|---|---|
| Questions | Answers |
| Who? | |
| What? | |
| Where? | |
| When? | |
| Why? | |
| How? | |

*Living Insights*

Are you sensing the value of the question/answer method of observation? There is no skill more helpful in Bible study than that of *observing* what is in the text.

• Let's continue our study of Romans by asking questions that arise from 10:16–11:36. Copy this chart and follow the same instructions given in study one. Before you begin, you may want to review what you have already discovered.

| Romans 10:16–11:36 | |
|---|---|
| Questions | Answers |
| Who? | |
| What? | |
| Where? | |
| When? | |
| Why? | |
| How? | |

# Straight Talk about Predestination
*Romans 9*

Few topics have sparked as many theological debates as the subject of divine predestination. Unfortunately, the heat generated by these debates has generally shed little light. In fact, the doctrine of predestination is still misunderstood and misapplied by many in our day. The best way to resolve the confusion that human opinion has produced is to return afresh to the biblical record. And among the many texts into which we could sink our teeth, none is more significant than Romans 9. In this single chapter, we are plummeted head-on into the very heart of predestination. Of course, this passage does not provide answers to all the questions we might have about predestination, but it does focus on some concepts that are central to our understanding of the doctrine. So let's pay close attention to what these verses teach and remain open to changing our view on predestination if need be.

## I. The Context of Romans 9.

Let's take a moment to get our bearings by (1) recalling the main argument of Romans, and (2) by looking at the issue that brings about Paul's discussion of predestination.

**A. The Argument of the Book.** In Romans Paul explains, defends, and applies the truth that *God imparts His righteousness to believing sinners.* Since chapter 9 occurs in this context, we can safely conclude that Paul's teaching on predestination concerns not just conversion but the entire plan of salvation. That is, we are predestined to a salvation-by-grace-through-faith type of plan that encompasses our whole lives.

**B. The Issue of the Jews.** The truth of this wonderful plan brings tears of grief to Paul's eyes as he considers how few of God's chosen people have accepted it: "I am telling the truth in Christ, I am not lying, my conscience bearing me witness in the Holy Spirit, that I have great sorrow and unceasing grief in my heart" (vv. 1–2). Paul adds to this that he would, if possible, give up his salvation in order to save some of his fellow Jews (v. 3)—those "to whom belongs the adoption as sons and the glory and the covenants and the giving of the Law and the temple service and the promises, whose are the fathers, and from whom is the Christ according to the flesh" (vv. 4–5a). With few exceptions, this divinely chosen and blessed people have rejected the gospel. This fact raises serious questions concerning the faithfulness of God and the validity of the gospel. Paul begins to answer these potential objections by appealing to the doctrine of predestination.

## II. Some Truths about Predestination.

In the remaining verses of Romans 9, Paul presents four facts about predestination and its relationship to the entire plan of salvation. Let's carefully examine each central truth.

A. **Predestination begins with the sovereign choice of God** (vv. 6–13). We are first told that God's promises to Israel have not failed because everyone who is a blood descendant of Abraham is not a beneficiary of the promise. In fact, the recipients of God's vows to Israel are those who are of Isaac's line (vv. 6–7). Isaac was one of two sons born to Abraham. God sovereignly chose him, not his brother Ishmael, to father the physical line of the Messiah (vv. 15–18, 21). Therefore, those who have accepted Christ are heirs of the promise that came through Isaac's heritage. We are next told about God's predetermined choice of Isaac's son, Jacob, to be the descendant through which the messianic seed would continue. Jacob was chosen for this role while still in Rebekah's womb with his twin brother Esau. God's election was made not on the basis of any works these two unborn twins had done but rather on the basis of His own sovereign decision (vv. 10–13).

B. **Predestination upholds the perfect character of God** (vv. 14–18). Because the Lord chose Isaac and Jacob instead of others, is His justice impugned? "May it never be!" retorts Paul (v. 14). Indeed, two illustrations from the Old Testament demonstrate that predestination displays God's justice *and* mercy. The first example concerns Moses. To him God said, " 'I will have mercy on whom I have mercy, and I will have compassion on whom I have compassion' " (v. 15). This verse shows that His sovereign choice "does not depend on the man who wills or the man who runs, but on God who has mercy" (v. 16). He does not consult anyone else about His choices or base them on the decisions of others. Rather, God's choices are dependent on His all-good and merciful nature *alone*. God's words to Pharaoh serve as a second illustration of this fact: " 'For this very purpose I raised you up, to demonstrate My power in you, and that My name might be proclaimed throughout the whole earth.' So then He has mercy on whom He desires, and He hardens whom He desires" (vv. 17–18). Although we make our decisions without complete information and a faultless character, the Lord makes His predeterminations with full knowledge and a perfect, all-just character.

C. **Predestination identifies the specific responsibility of God** (vv. 19–23). In response to what Paul has said so far, one might think: If the Lord exercises mercy or judgment on whomever He so chooses, then He has no concrete basis on which to fault man for sin. After all, who can possibly resist His will if He has predetermined for man to sin (v. 19)? Paul answers this objection with an illustration: "The thing molded will not say to the molder, 'Why did you make me like this,' will it? Or does not the potter have a right over the clay, to make from the same lump one vessel for honorable use, and another for common use?" (vv. 20b–21). So that we do not misunderstand Paul's answer, we need to briefly recall some biblical truths about sin. After the Fall of man in the Garden of Eden (Gen. 3), the only clay God had to work with was marked by sin. He did not cause man to sin then, and He does not make anyone disobey today (James 1:13–15). Human beings are responsible for their own wrongdoing. However, from the marred clay of sinful humanity, God takes on the responsibility for shaping individuals in varied ways. And as the Creator, it is His prerogative to do so. Therefore, He had every right to choose Isaac instead of Ishmael, or Jacob rather than Esau. Besides, they were born sinners and therefore were totally undeserving of any mercy God might choose to show them. Thus, the very fact that He decided to select any of them to play a roll in His salvation plan is absolutely amazing. We too are undeserving of God's grace. But because the Lord is rich in mercy and lovingkindness, He has decided to save those who accept Jesus Christ by faith and to shape them into Christ's image. How great is the Lord! He's so worthy to be praised!

**D. Predestination defends the consistent plan of God** (vv. 24–33). The Lord's prearranged program has always been that salvation, from conversion to glorification, is by grace through faith alone. Therefore, those who have tried to earn their salvation have been denied it, while those who have exercised faith have been granted it. In the latter verses of Romans 9, Paul explains the main reason why most Jews have not been saved—they have chosen to pursue works, not faith, in a plan that recognizes faith alone. The Gentiles, on the other hand, "who did not pursue [that is, work for] righteousness, attained righteousness, even the righteousness which is by faith" (v. 30). Thus, nothing is wrong with God's plan; it has been operating consistently. The fault lies with those who try to work for salvation rather than accept it by faith alone.

## III. The Response of the Hearer.

There are three ways we could respond to the teaching on predestination in Romans.

**A. We could totally reject it.** Rather than embracing these truths, we could adopt the view that God does nothing in regard to salvation, while we do everything.

**B. We could take it to another extreme.** That is, we could conclude that God does everything in the salvation process, while we do nothing.

**C. We could accept it as it is.** Predestination does not negate human responsibility; it simply places our role where it should be—under the authority and sovereignty of God. He has predecided in His infinite mercy that we can freely come to Him and become righteous by faith alone. The choice we must make is whether we are going to adopt His way of salvation, or try our own method. But as He has predetermined, only His way leads to everlasting life, while ours can end only in everlasting death.

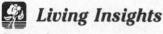 *Living Insights*

"What shall we say then? *There is no injustice with God, is there?* May it never be!" (Rom. 9:14, emphasis added). In the verses that follow this declaration, we find a marvelous defense of the perfect character of God. The whole passage conveys the fact that God is very different from us.

- We can discover the answer to this question by examining the many attributes of God and comparing them with what we know about ourselves. So with the help of a concordance and a book on Bible doctrine, do some study on one or more of God's characteristics listed below. Be warned, however, that this study could change your life! Why? Because when we know what God is like, we have a better picture of ourselves and our desperate need for Him.

| The Character of God | | |
|---|---|---|
| Divine Attributes | Scripture References | Definitions |
| Spirit | | |
| Infinite | | |
| Immutable | | |
| Eternal | | |
| Omnipotent | | |
| Omniscient | | |
| Omnipresent | | |
| Good | | |
| Love | | |
| Merciful | | |
| Just | | |
| Righteous | | |
| Holy | | |
| Wrathful | | |
| Faithful | | |
| Truth | | |
| Sovereign | | |
| Perfect | | |

*Living Insights*

Are you having trouble grasping the teaching of Romans 9? Well, remember the words from Proverbs: "In abundance of counselors there is victory" (11:14b). Gather together your family and/or friends and *discuss* the issues raised in the chapter. Use the following suggestions as guidelines in your discussion.

- In Romans 9:1–5, Paul is very disturbed. Read these verses, and then explain why this is so. Do you feel uneasy because some of your friends or family members don't know Christ? Talk about that burden, then pray specifically for those who concern you the most.
- Read Romans 9:6–13 several times aloud. What stands out as being most important and/or difficult to you? Why? Does it seem strange that a set of twins could be so completely different? Pay close attention to the eleventh verse—particularly to what it says about God's role in the whole affair.
- The issue about God's justice comes to the surface in Romans 9:14–18. Read this passage carefully. You might even want to use the Living Bible or another version. Talk about God's justice in light of verse 18. Don't feel badly if you have difficulty fully understanding it. Even the most knowledgeable Bible scholars wrestle with this subject. Pause and read Romans 11:33–36, letting these words remind you of a comforting truth.
- In Romans 9:19–24 there is a lovely word picture used by the Apostle Paul. Can you identify it? Now flip the pages back to Jeremiah 18:1–6 and read it as well. Take some time to think it over. Put yourself on the Potter's wheel and share at least one area in which God has been working in your life. Be open and honest; even be willing to admit that He isn't through with you yet.
- The response of the Gentiles is contrasted with the response of the Jews in Romans 9:30–33. State what the difference is according to these words from Romans. Talk about how that very same difference exists *today*. Why do you suppose so many pursue a righteousness-by-works lifestyle? Talk about your own tendency at times to live like that and consider what you need to do in order to walk more consistently by faith.

# Straight Talk about Responsibility

*Romans 10*

The all-too-common response to Romans 9 goes something like this: "Because God is sovereign, I am not responsible for my actions. My lost and sinful condition is God's fault, not mine. I'm exactly what God has made me to be!" Romans 10 assaults this false conclusion head-on. Without retreating one inch from the truth of predestination, this section of Scripture puts the responsibility for man's sinful, lost condition where it belongs—squarely in man's lap. Human beings cannot hide behind divine sovereignty in an attempt to excuse their sinful state. Their willful rejection of the gospel is the reason they are not saved. Romans 10 clarifies that point without apology.

## I. A Preview of Responsibility.

Those who have refused to place their faith in Jesus Christ are responsible for their unbelief. The tenth chapter of Romans demonstrates this fact with reference to the nation of Israel. Let's take a general survey of what this chapter teaches before we probe into its details.

### A. Message of the Chapter.

The central thought of Romans 10 can be summarized in a single sentence: *God has rejected Israel because her people have rejected His Messiah, Jesus Christ.* In fact, that is the only reason God ever rejects anyone.

### B. Development of the Logic.

The message of this chapter is supported by four facts. The first one is that *the good news about the Messiah was within Israel's reach* (10:8). The Jews had the Scriptures for centuries. And because God's salvation plan was clearly revealed in His Word, Israel had every opportunity to repent and be saved. The second fact is that *the gospel of Christ is offered to all* (vv. 11–13). Salvation by faith is made available to everyone, not simply the elect. Christ died for the whole world (John 3:16). This includes those who God knew would die without ever trusting in His Son (2 Pet. 2:1–9). Third, *the gospel is not accepted by all* (Rom. 10:16). Many Jews and Gentiles have refused to believe in Christ as the Messiah. And fourth, *the gospel continues to be offered to all,* even in spite of persistent unbelief (Rom. 10:21). So in regard to Israel, the Lord says, " 'All the day long I have stretched out My hands to a disobedient and obstinate people' " (cf. Isa. 65:1–2a). Praise God, He still reaches out to us in the same gracious way! For unless He did, no one would be saved.

## II. An Analysis of Responsibility.

Now that we have a basic overview of Romans 10, let's take some time to study its particulars.

  **A. The Transition** (Rom. 9:30–10:7). The introduction to chapter 10 is found in the last few verses of chapter 9. There we learn that the Jews who tried to earn righteousness by keeping the Mosaic Law failed to achieve it, while the Gentiles who reached out for God's righteousness by faith received it (9:30–33). But this fact did not stop Paul from praying for his fellow kinsmen (10:1). His greatest desire was for the salvation of the Jews, even though he knew that they were "seeking to establish their own [righteousness]" (v. 3) instead of embracing God's plan by faith. Because the Jews refused to submit to God, they became victims of their own pride. This Jewish brand of self-righteousness was emphatically condemned by Jesus in Matthew 23:13–36. And after He delivered a strong rebuke, He laid the responsibility for the Jews' unbelief at their doorstep. Notice what He said: " 'O Jerusalem, Jerusalem, who kills the prophets and stones those who are sent to her! How often I wanted to gather your children together, the way a hen gathers her chicks under her wings, and *you were unwilling*' " (Matt. 23:37, emphasis added). Although they repeatedly heard the gospel message, they freely rejected it.

  **B. An Exposition** (Rom. 10:8–21). In this section, Paul squarely sets his sights on human responsibility in relation to salvation. Let's look at each main thought he develops.

  1. **Because the gospel is available, people are responsible** (vv. 8–10). Salvation from sin is offered to all as a divine gift. How can it be received? Paul tells us with crystal clarity: "If you confess with your mouth Jesus as Lord, and believe in your heart that God raised Him from the dead, you shall be saved; for with the heart man believes, resulting in righteousness, and with the mouth he confesses, resulting in salvation" (vv. 9–10). It is obvious from these words that the responsibility to accept the gift of salvation rests on man, not anyone else.

  2. **Because the offer is universal, every person is responsible** (vv. 11–15). Any individual confronted with the salvation message is held accountable by God to accept or reject it. And whoever embraces the gospel by faith *will* be saved. On the flip side of this is another responsibility. The person who has placed his or her trust in Christ is obligated and encouraged to proclaim Him to others. This truth is conveyed in these words: "How then shall they call upon Him in whom they have not believed? And how shall they believe in Him whom they have not heard? And how

63

shall they hear without a preacher? And how shall they preach unless they are sent? Just as it is written, 'How beautiful are the feet of those who bring glad tidings of good things!'" (vv. 14–15). What a responsibility and a privilege we have!

3. **Because rejection is predictable, the unsaved are responsible** (vv. 16–20). Even under the ministry of the great prophet Isaiah, many Jews chose to reject "the word of Christ" (vv. 16–17). The problem was not that they had failed to hear the gospel message, but that they were willfully rebellious against God and His salvation plan. Since that time, nothing has changed. Some people will hear the gospel and persist in freely rejecting it.

4. **Because God is faithful, people are continually responsible** (v. 21). The Lord never gave up on Israel, and He never will. He has not changed. He persists in reaching out to people even when they continue in their unbelief.

## III. A Summary of Responsibility.

As we reflect on what this text has to say, we can discover three truths that sum it all up.

A. **The Christian is responsible to pray for and share his or her faith with non-Christians.**

B. **The non-Christian is responsible to accept or reject God's free gift of salvation.**

C. **The Lord is responsible to save whoever comes to Him through Christ by faith alone.**

 *Living Insights*

**Study One** ▬▬▬▬▬▬▬▬▬▬▬▬▬▬▬▬▬▬▬▬▬▬▬▬▬▬▬▬▬

This lesson presents some straight talk about the responsibility of mankind in relationship to God's salvation plan. Let's take this opportunity to see how the teaching in Romans 10 applies to each one of us.

● Earlier in this study guide we tried our hand at *paraphrasing.* Let's do it again with Romans 10. Write out those twenty-one verses in your own words. As you do this, get inside the words on paper and sense the feelings that permeate the text. Also, use this exercise as an opportunity to personalize the passage. For example, try replacing such words as *man, they,* and *them* with your own name. This process is bound to give you a deeper appreciation of *your* responsibility in God's salvation plan.

*Living Insights*

Who has *beautiful feet* in your life? Who was the person who shared with you the message of salvation? Was it your parent, friend, teacher, pastor, or someone else?

• You can honor the person who led you to Christ. One way is to pause and pray for that person right now. Another way is to write a note letting this individual know that he or she is in your thoughts. How about sending a thoughtful gift? Perhaps something that has special significance to your friendship would be best. Spend a few minutes thinking about it, and then follow it up by honoring this important person.

# The Jew: Cast Off or Set Aside?

*Romans 11:1–14*

In Romans 9, we learned that God chose Israel to be the recipient of great blessings. We discovered in the tenth chapter of this letter that God has since rejected Israel because she refused to accept her Messiah, Jesus Christ. Now, in chapter 11, we will see that God has not yet finished with Israel. Indeed, His predetermined plan involves the future redemption and full inheritance of the promises He made to her.

## I. Let's understand the issues.

Paul begins Romans 11 with a question: "I say then, God has not rejected His people, has He?" (v. 1a). In order for us to understand what is being asked, we must resolve the following issues:

**A. The Identification Issue.** To what or whom does the phrase "His people" refer? We know from Romans 9:6–8 and 11:5 that it could not refer to all Jews, since some have been saved by God's grace through faith. Therefore, the phrase must denote the nation of the Jews, Israel.

**B. The Rejection Issue.** What could be meant by the word *rejected?* In the context of chapter 11, it could mean that God has permanently cast off and forgotten about Israel, or that He has temporarily set her aside. In the question Paul poses, the first explanation is meant. But notice that he totally rejects the idea that the Lord has forever turned His back on Israel (v. 1). In fact, Paul begins to argue from the evidence that Israel has a magnificent future in store for her. In the meantime, however, she is experiencing the discipline of her King.

## II. Let's discover the plan.

How does Paul support his case that God has not abandoned Israel? He does this by giving four pieces of evidence. Each one demonstrates that God has set aside Israel only temporarily. He then supplies us with two reasons that shed some revealing light as to why God has chosen to deal with Israel in this way.

**A. Four Proofs** (vv. 1b–10). Let's examine them as they appear in the text.

1. **Paul Himself** (v. 1b). If God had permanently cast off the entire nation of Israel, then no Jew could possibly be saved. However, Paul was a Jew, as these words reveal: "For I too am an Israelite, a descendant of Abraham, of the tribe of Benjamin." And he had been converted by faith to Christianity (Acts 9). Therefore, God must not have turned away from His chosen nation.

2. **God's Eternal Plan** (v. 2a). Here we are told that "God has not rejected His people whom He foreknew." Before Israel was a nation, God had sovereignly selected her to fulfill a special role in His eternal plan. He has chosen to bestow His love on her in a unique way. And what He decides to do, He accomplishes. These words could not make it more clear: "From the standpoint of the gospel they [the Jews] are enemies for your sake, but from the standpoint of God's choice they are beloved for the sake of the fathers; *for the gifts and the calling of God are irrevocable*" (Rom. 11:28–29, emphasis added). The Lord has called Israel to be the beneficiary of tremendous blessing. He will not change His mind or take back His promises. He is immutably faithful!

3. **A Chosen Remnant** (vv. 2b–6). This piece of evidence is drawn from an incident in the life of Elijah, one of God's greatest prophets. After he had conquered and destroyed the prophets of Baal through God's miraculous power, he became terrified of Jezebel's threat to kill him. So he ran away and cried out to God, asking Him to take his life. In his prayer, Elijah claimed to be the only believer left in Israel. But God's response set him straight: " 'I have kept for Myself seven thousand men who have not bowed the knee to Baal' " (Rom. 11:4; cf. 1 Kings 18:1–19:18). Elijah may have felt all alone, but he was not Israel's sole surviving convert. "In the same way then," Paul adds, "there has also come to be at the present time a remnant according to God's gracious choice" (Rom. 11:5). Just as there were other saved Jews in Elijah's day, so there are saved Jews today. God has not abandoned Israel; He has graciously selected a remnant of Jews who have embraced the Messiah by faith (v. 6).

4. **The Nature of Discipline** (vv. 7–10). In these verses we discover that those Jews who have not exercised faith in Jesus Christ have been "hardened" by God. That is, the Lord has made them insensitive to the spiritual matters of grace. Having rejected salvation by faith in favor of that by works, they have been put in a spiritual stupor by God as a measure of discipline. This does not mean that Israel will be under the disciplinary hand of God forever. Indeed, discipline is always temporary, and it is inflicted for purposes of good, not evil (Heb. 12:10–11). Thus, the very nature of discipline shows that God has something better planned for Israel's future.

**B. Two Reasons** (vv. 11-14). Why has God chosen to temporarily set Israel aside? One reason is so that salvation would come to the Gentiles (v. 11b). The sovereign Lord has used Israel's rejection of the Messiah to bring the gospel to non-Jews. The second reason is so that unsaved Jews might be moved to jealousy and, as a result, embrace the gospel by faith (vv. 11b-14). In addition, Paul adds, if "their transgression be riches for the world and their failure be riches for the Gentiles, how much more will their fulfillment be!" (v. 12). God will one day honor all of the glorious promises that He made to Israel. Indeed, He will make their future exceedingly richer than their past.

## III. Let's appropriate the message.

Two principles stand out as we seek to apply the truths in this chapter.

**A. Unlike man, God does His best work through a remnant.** We are enamored by great numbers of people being converted to Christ and used by God. The Lord, however, often accomplishes His work through a small group of people who have committed themselves to Him no matter what.

**B. Unlike the world, God keeps His promises.** Even though we will often fail Him, He will never fail us. What He says He will do will certainly be accomplished. We can count on that!

 *Living Insights*

**Study One** ▬▬▬▬▬▬▬▬▬▬▬▬▬▬▬▬▬▬▬▬▬▬▬▬

Romans 9-11 contains a careful blending of God's sovereignty and man's responsibility. Chapter 11 zeros in on the Jews. Using these people as our focal point, copy the following questions into your notebook and proceed to discover the answers.

- Based on Romans 9, how would you describe Israel's past?
- Based on Romans 10, how would you describe Israel's present?
- Based on Romans 11, how would you describe Israel's future?
- When we talk about Israel, are we speaking about the nation or individuals?
- Has God permanently cast off Israel?
- Does the gospel still apply to the Jews?
- Based on Romans 11, where do the Gentiles fit into God's plan?

*Living Insights*

The familiar story of Elijah and his lonely struggle is set forth in Romans 11:2–5. We know from this passage that he experienced deep discouragement much like the rest of us.

● Read the story of Elijah in 1 Kings 19. Why did Elijah feel the way he did? Was he *really* all alone? Let's chart out some insights you've gleaned over the years on *overcoming discouragement*. Be sure to include how you were victorious.

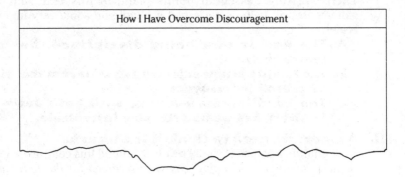

How I Have Overcome Discouragement

# Horticultural Ethics

*Romans 11:15–29*

These fifteen verses in the middle of Romans 11 are difficult, but not impossible, to understand. They will demand our full attention as we begin to examine their context and the metaphors they utilize. So let's roll up our sleeves and dig in! The Lord has a great deal to teach us through this passage.

**I. Question: "What in the world is this saying?"**

There are three essential points made in this text. And these statements will help us get a better handle on some very important issues.

  **A. The Jew is now being disciplined, but only temporarily.**

  **B. The Gentile is now enjoying salvation, but that yields no reason for smugness or pride.**

  **C. The Lord is now working with both Jews and Gentiles, and we find His plan inscrutable.**

**II. Answer: We need to think this through.**

Each point in Romans 11:15–29 revolves around this central idea: *What Gentile Christians now enjoy was once reserved for the Jews, and in the future it will be theirs again.* This controlling thought comes through in the four key characteristics that follow. Let's take some time to study each one.

  **A. The Context** (vv. 11–15). These verses inform us that the unsaved Jews, though hardened, are not irretrievably lost. As a nation, they have been temporarily set aside so that the Gentiles might gain what the Jews have lost. In other words, by the transgression of the Jews "salvation has come to the Gentiles" (v. 11)...but even this act of God has been performed for the sake of the Jews. For through the salvation of the Gentiles, the Jews are being provoked to jealousy so that they might be saved as well (vv. 11b, 13–15). God longs for the Jews to repent of their unbelief and become recipients of the blessings that were originally theirs.

  **B. The Metaphors** (vv. 16–17). Paul uses two word pictures to illustrate his point.

  1. **The first one relates to baking:** "If the first piece of dough be holy, the lump is also" (v. 16a). In order to better grasp the meaning of this, we need some background information. When a Jewish farmer raised a grain crop, he would cut off the first shoot or sheath and bring it to a priest. Under the Mosaic Law, this crop sample was to be given to God as a first-fruit offering. In this way, the entire crop was

70

recognized as a provision from God. The Jews followed a similar procedure when they began to bake goods made from the grain crops they had planted and cultivated. Thus, the first piece of dough was given as a peace offering. It was simply a sample of all that would be cooked that season for God's glory (cf. Num. 15:1–21). Given this background material, it is not difficult to understand the meaning of Paul's illustration. The "first piece of dough" refers to Abraham, Isaac, and Jacob, who were all recipients of righteousness through faith. The "lump" represents the nation of Israel. So the truth being taught is that if the first generations of Israel were set apart to God, then so is the entire nation. The Jews always were, presently are, and forever will be God's chosen people.

2. **The second one relates to gardening:** "And if the root be holy, the branches are too. But if some of the branches were broken off, and you, being a wild olive, were grafted in among them and became partaker with them of the rich root of the olive tree . . ." (Rom. 11:16b–17). With regard to Israel, the "root" stands for Abraham—the physical and spiritual father of the nation. And since he was set apart by God for a special purpose, all his descendants have also been set apart by the Lord. But some of his Jewish descendants have been passed over because of their unbelief in the Messiah. As a consequence, non-Jews have been grafted onto the Abrahamic tree and thereby have been offered the same opportunity for salvation that the Jews have been given. And when they become partakers with believing Jews by trusting in Christ by faith, they reap the same benefits of salvation that the Jewish believers receive.

C. **The Warning** (vv. 18–22). In these verses, the warning is directed toward Gentile Christians. All non-Jewish believers are told not to be arrogant because of their new position alongside Jewish believers; namely, as joint-heirs of God's promises. In addition, Gentile Christians should remember their non-Christian days when they were "separate from Christ, excluded from the commonwealth of Israel, and strangers to the covenants of promise, having no hope and without God in the world" (Eph. 2:12b). Thus, Gentile believers should be grateful and loving toward their Jewish brethren.

D. **The Plan** (vv. 23–29). As these verses in Romans relate, "A partial hardening has happened to Israel until the fulness of the Gentiles has come in; and thus all Israel will be saved" (vv. 25b–26a). God's plan is that once the elect Gentiles have

71

been saved, Israel will be established as a holy nation with Christ as her Ruler. In the meantime, the Jews largely remain insensitive to the claims of the gospel even though they are the beloved of God (v. 28).

## III. Response: "All right, now it's clear."

With these thoughts behind us, we can now understand the message of this passage more fully. The following three statements aptly summarize the instruction found in Romans 11:15-29.

**A. The Jew is currently hardened but ultimately beloved.**

**B. The Gentile is spiritually honored but personally undeserving.**

**C. The Lord is severe to some but fair to all.**

 *Living Insights*

**Study One** ▬▬▬▬▬▬▬▬▬▬▬▬▬▬▬▬▬▬▬▬▬▬▬▬

In order for the Apostle Paul to clarify the main idea of this passage, he uses *two metaphors*—baking and gardening. But these will only help explain the meaning if you understand the processes involved in these activities. So put on your chef's hat and grab a shovel . . . here we go!

● Choose one of these metaphors. Check a concordance for all the Scripture references that relate to either baking or gardening. You'll probably discover that there is more information on the topic of gardening than on the subject of baking. In the right column of the chart below, jot down a statement explaining what the passages tell you about each metaphor.

| Meaningful Metaphors—Baking and Gardening | |
|---|---|
| Scripture References | Statements of Explanation |
|  |  |

*Living Insights*

We're quickly approaching the end of this section of Romans. So many rich nuggets of truth have been uncovered in these middle chapters that it would be good for us to appropriate them through prayer.

● Flip through the pages in your study guide and remind yourself of the many truths you have learned. Then talk to God about your struggles, your walk in the Spirit, your battle with the flesh, and the host of other things that may come to mind. Ask God to help you deal with these areas in your life.

# Unsearchable, Unfathomable, Unmatched!

*Romans 11:30–36*

The loftiest mountain peaks of biblical truth are those that declare God's praises. In the last section of Romans 11, we find just such a mountain summit. It is perhaps the greatest of all doxologies recorded in Holy Scripture. This doxology closes a profound set of chapters that are related directly to God's plan for Israel and indirectly to His program for Gentiles. Let's approach these final verses with the reverence and humility they deserve.

## I. The Mercy of God: *How Unsearchable!*

In Romans 11:30–32, Paul presents us with a succinct summary of the Jew-Gentile issue he has been discussing. There we find him rightly focusing on the unsearchable mercy of God.

**A. To the Gentiles** (v. 30). Paul first refers to Gentiles by summing up their background in three words—"disobedient to God." Elsewhere in Scripture he expands on their biography by portraying the Gentiles as a spiritually barren people. Reflectively consider what he says:

> And you [Gentiles] were dead in your trespasses and sins, in which you formerly walked according to the course of this world, according to the prince of the power of the air, of the spirit that is now working in the sons of disobedience. . . . Therefore remember, that formerly you, the Gentiles in the flesh . . . remember that you were at that time separate from Christ, excluded from the commonwealth of Israel, and strangers to the covenants of promise, having no hope and without God in the world (Eph. 2:1–2, 11a, 12).

In such a miserable and wretched state, Gentiles have only one hope—the mercy of God. And praise be to the Lord that He exercises compassion toward rebellious Gentiles! But why has He shown them such mercy? For what reason has He so graciously grafted them into a salvation plan that they do not deserve? The reason, says Paul, is the disobedience of the Jews (Rom. 11:30). Because they have rejected God's appointed Messiah and have sought to earn their salvation by works rather than by faith, God has hardened them against the truth and temporarily set them aside. As a consequence, He has made available to the Gentiles what was formerly offered to the Jews—His entire salvation plan.

**B. To the Jews** (v. 31). Does God's outstretched hand to the Gentiles mean that He has abandoned the Jews? Not at all! The Lord's mercy has been manifested to the Gentiles so that through them the Jews "may now be shown mercy." Earlier in Romans 11, Paul personalized this truth in these words: "Inasmuch then as I am an apostle of Gentiles, I magnify my ministry, if somehow I might move to jealousy my fellow countrymen and save some of them" (vv. 13b–14).

**C. To All** (v. 32). Here we learn that Jews and Gentiles alike have been "shut up . . . in disobedience [so] that He might show mercy to all." The Greek term translated *shut up* means "to shut in on all sides." The word was often used to describe fish caught in a net, or animals stuck in a trap. The text is teaching that all human beings have been caught in the trap of sin; thus, there is no difference between Jews and Gentiles. Furthermore, the only key that unlocks this trap is God's mercy. By sending His Son to die for all sinners, the Lord has impartially exercised His abundant compassion. All we need to do is reach out to Him with our empty hands and grasp His unsearchable mercy through Jesus Christ.

## II. The Mind of God: *How Unfathomable!*

Beginning in verse 33, Paul breaks into a doxology that exalts the infinite mind of God. It's as though he has reached the highest mountain peak and, in the throes of its ineffable magnificence, attempted to verbally express the deep awe he is experiencing. Let's try to enter into his admiration as we make our way through verses 33–35.

**A. Exclamation Needing No Proof** (v. 33). In a burst of praise, Paul writes: "Oh, the depth of the riches both of the wisdom and knowledge of God! How unsearchable are His judgments and unfathomable His ways!" In other words, Paul is exclaiming the boundless extent of the Lord's understanding. His wisdom and knowledge are immeasurable. He knows everything about what was, is, and will be. He knows what is both possible and impossible. And He has the ability to apply His infinite knowledge with perfect skill and precision. No wonder Paul declares that God's ways are *unfathomable*—incapable of being traced by anyone but the Lord. His activities defy our complete understanding.

**B. Questions Needing No Answer** (vv. 34–35). Flowing from Paul's exclamation are three questions—all of which assume a negative answer. First, "Who has known the mind of the Lord?" Since He is infinite, no creature could ever comprehend His mind. Second, "Who became His counselor?" Because God knows all things, including how to wisely apply His knowledge, no creature could ever act as His consultant. And third, "Who has first given to Him that it might be paid back to him again?" Since He is the boundless Creator, Sustainer, Redeemer, and Provider of all, no creature could ever give Him anything that would put Him in debt.

### III. The Majesty of God: *How Unmatched!*

Paul closes his proclamation of praise with a declaration of God's incomparable majesty.

   **A. Temporal Events** (v. 36a). Paul states, "For from Him and through Him and to Him are all things." We might clarify the meaning of this sentence by paraphrasing it in this way: "God is the ultimate source, perfect channel, and final goal of all good things" (cf. James 1:16–17). The Lord is even able to "cause all things to work together for good" (Rom. 8:28). This encompasses every aspect of our lives, including our mates, families, jobs, churches, and daily occurrences. He is in control, and we need to live in accord with that fact.

   **B. Eternal Glory** (v. 36b). The doxology ends with a proclamation of the ultimate honor, central focus, and radiant magnificence of God: "To Him be the glory forever. Amen."

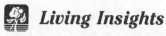 *Living Insights*

Let's take some time to look back over our study together. Have you been motivated to walk by grace? How have these lessons been helpful in learning to live by the Spirit instead of the flesh?

● The following chart includes the titles of our sixteen lessons. Let's use this time to review the most noteworthy truth you learned from each study. As you look back through your Bible, study guide, and notebook, jot down the truths in the right column.

| Learning to Walk by Grace | |
|---|---|
| Message Titles | Meaningful Truths |
| Dying to Live | |
| Whose Slave Are You? | |
| Portrait of a Struggling Christian | |
| Free Spirit | |
| Talking about Walking | |
| A Spirit-Controlled Mind-set | |
| The Glory and the Groan | |
| Providence Made Practical | |
| Providence Made Personal | |
| We Overwhelmingly Conquer | |
| God, the Jew, and You Too | |
| Straight Talk about Predestination | |
| Straight Talk about Responsibility | |
| The Jew: Cast Off or Set Aside? | |
| Horticultural Ethics | |
| Unsearchable, Unfathomable, Unmatched! | |

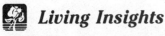 *Living Insights*

Let's continue the process of review. This time we will change our focus from truth to application. It's important to make the extra effort to appropriate these lessons in our lives.

- Copy the following chart into your notebook. As you browse through the material we've covered in this study, search out the most memorable application you made from each lesson. Jot down each one in the right column.

| Learning to Walk by Grace | |
| --- | --- |
| Message Titles | Memorable Applications |
| Dying to Live | |
| Whose Slave Are You? | |
| Portrait of a Struggling Christian | |
| Free Spirit | |
| Talking about Walking | |
| A Spirit-Controlled Mind-set | |
| The Glory and the Groan | |
| Providence Made Practical | |
| Providence Made Personal | |
| We Overwhelmingly Conquer | |
| God, the Jew, and You Too | |
| Straight Talk about Predestination | |
| Straight Talk about Responsibility | |
| The Jew: Cast Off or Set Aside? | |
| Horticultural Ethics | |
| Unsearchable, Unfathomable, Unmatched! | |

# Books for Probing Further

We have learned a great deal about what it means to walk by grace. Romans 6–11 has supplied answers to the questions we often pose and solutions to the problems we usually encounter. However, among the many subjects and issues we have dealt with, there may be some into which you would like to probe further. With this in mind, we have pulled together several resources on some of the more significant areas that we have covered. For your convenience, we have listed them below under their respective headings. Our hope is that you will use these sources not merely to help you think by grace but to motivate you to live by grace.

## I. Learning about God.

Bavinck, Herman. *The Doctrine of God*. Translated, edited, and outlined by William Hendriksen. Grand Rapids: Baker Book House, 1977.

Baxter, J. Sidlow. *Majesty: The God You Should Know*. San Bernardino: Here's Life Publishers, 1984.

Charnock, Stephen. *The Existence and Attributes of God*. 2 vols. Grand Rapids: Baker Book House, 1979.

France, R. T. *The Living God*. Downers Grove: InterVarsity Press, 1970.

Hocking, David L. *The Nature of God in Plain Language*. Waco: Word Books, 1984.

Lewis, C. S. *Mere Christianity*. Revised edition. New York: Macmillan Publishing Co., Inc., 1952.

Packer, J. I. *Knowing God*. Downers Grove: InterVarsity Press, 1973.

Shedd, William G. T. *Dogmatic Theology*. Vol. 1. Reprint edition. Minneapolis: Klock & Klock Christian Publishers, 1979.

Strauss, Richard L. *The Joy of Knowing God*. Neptune: Loizeaux Brothers, Inc., 1984.

Thiessen, Henry Clarence. *Lectures in Systematic Theology*. Revised by Vernon D. Doerksen. Grand Rapids: William B. Eerdmans Publishing Co., 1979.

Tozer, A. W. *The Knowledge of the Holy*. New York: Harper & Brothers, 1961.

## II. Learning about the Holy Spirit.

Chafer, Lewis Sperry. *He That Is Spiritual*. Revised edition. Grand Rapids: Zondervan Publishing House, 1967.

Cumming, James Elder. *"Through the Eternal Spirit": A Biblical Study on the Holy Spirit*. Minneapolis: Bethany Fellowship, 1965.

Kuyper, Abraham. *The Work of the Holy Spirit*. Reprint edition. Translated by Reverend Henri De Vries. Introduction by Benjamin B. Warfield. Grand Rapids: William B. Eerdmans Publishing Co., 1979.

Morris, Leon. *Spirit of the Living God*. Downers Grove: InterVarsity Press, 1960.

Owen, John. *The Holy Spirit, His Gifts and Power.* Reprint edition. Grand Rapids: Kregel Publications, 1960.

Pache, René. *The Person and Work of the Holy Spirit.* Chicago: Moody Press, 1954.

Packer, J. I. *Keep in Step with the Spirit.* Old Tappan: Fleming H. Revell Co., 1984.

Ryrie, Charles Caldwell. *The Holy Spirit.* Chicago: Moody Press, 1965.

Thomas, W. H. Griffith. *The Holy Spirit of God.* Reprint edition. Grand Rapids: William B. Eerdmans Publishing Co., 1963.

Walvoord, John F. *The Holy Spirit.* 3d edition. Grand Rapids: Zondervan Publishing House, 1958.

### III. Learning about Predestination.

Anselm, Saint. *Trinity, Incarnation, and Redemption: Theological Treatises.* Revised edition. Edited and translated by Jasper Hopkins and Herbert W. Richardson. New York: Harper Torchbooks, 1970.

Berkouwer, G. C. *The Providence of God.* Translated by Lewis Smedes. Studies in Dogmatics. Grand Rapids: William B. Eerdmans Publishing Co., 1952.

Forster, Roger T., and Marston, V. Paul. *God's Strategy in Human History.* Foreword by F. F. Bruce. Wheaton: Tyndale House Publishers, Inc., 1973.

Geisler, Norman L. "Freedom, Free Will, and Determinism." In *Evangelical Dictionary of Theology.* Edited by Walter A. Elwell. Grand Rapids: Baker Book House, 1984.

Geisler, Norman L. "God, Evil, and Dispensations." In *Walvoord: A Tribute.* Edited by Donald K. Campbell. Chicago: Moody Press, 1982.

Geisler, Norman L. "Man's Destiny: Free or Forced?" *Christian Scholar's Review* 9:2 (1979), pp. 99–109.

Packer, J. I. *Evangelism and the Sovereignty of God.* Downers Grove: InterVarsity Press, 1961.

Pinnock, Clark H., editor. *Grace Unlimited.* Minneapolis: Bethany Fellowship, Inc., 1975.

Thiessen, Henry C. *Lectures in Systematic Theology.* Revised by Vernon D. Doerksen. Grand Rapids: William B. Eerdmans Publishing Co., 1979.

Yohn, Rick. *Living Securely in an Unstable World: God's Solution to Man's Dilemma.* Portland: Multnomah Press, 1985.

### IV. Learning about Suffering.

Attlee, Rosemary. *William's Story: A Mother's Account of Her Son's Struggle against Cancer.* Wheaton: Harold Shaw Publishers, 1983.

Baker, Don. *Pain's Hidden Purpose: Finding Perspective in the Midst of Suffering.* Portland: Multnomah Press, 1984.

Barber, Cyril J. *Ruth: An Expositional Commentary.* Chicago: Moody Press, 1983.

Bayly, Joseph. *The Last Thing We Talk About.* Revised edition. Elgin: David C. Cook Publishing Co., 1973.

Brand, Paul, and Yancey, Philip. *Healing.* Portland: Multnomah Press, 1984.

Britton, Janet. *To Live Each Moment: One Woman's Struggle against Cancer.* Downers Grove: InterVarsity Press, 1984.

D'Arcy, Paula. *Where the Wind Begins.* Wheaton: Harold Shaw Publishers, 1984.

Glaphré. *When the Pieces Don't Fit . . . God Makes the Difference.* Foreword by Gloria Gaither. Grand Rapids: Zondervan Publishing House, 1984.

Graham, Billy. *Till Armageddon: A Perspective on Suffering.* Waco: Word Books, 1981.

Hawley, Gloria Hope. *Laura's Legacy: A Living Testament of Love.* Nashville: Impact Books, 1982.

Hawley, Gloria Hope. *Laura's Psalm.* Nashville: Impact Books, 1981.

Hazelip, Harold. *Lord, Help Me When I'm Hurting.* Grand Rapids: Baker Book House, 1984.

Kaiser, Walter C., Jr. *A Biblical Approach to Personal Suffering.* Chicago: Moody Press, 1982.

Lewis, C. S. *A Grief Observed.* New York: The Seabury Press, 1961.

Lewis, C. S. *The Problem of Pain.* New York: Macmillan Publishing Co., Inc., 1962.

Manning, Doug. *Comforting Those Who Grieve: A Guide for Helping Others.* San Francisco: Harper & Row, Publishers, 1985.

Means, James E. *A Tearful Celebration.* Portland: Multnomah Press, 1985.

Richards, Larry, and Johnson, Paul. *Death and the Caring Community: Ministering to the Terminally Ill.* A Critical Concern Book. Portland: Multnomah Press, 1980.

Strauss, Lehman. *In God's Waiting Room: Learning through Suffering.* Chicago: Moody Press, 1985.

Swindoll, Charles R. *When Your Comfort Zone Gets the Squeeze.* Fullerton: Insight for Living, 1985.

Swindoll, Chuck. *For Those Who Hurt.* Portland: Multnomah Press, 1977.

Ton, Mary Ellen. *The Flames Shall Not Consume You.* Elgin: David C. Cook Publishing Co., 1982.

Vredevelt, Pam W. *Empty Arms.* Portland: Multnomah Press, 1984.

Wiersbe, Warren W. *Why Us? When Bad Things Happen to God's People.* Old Tappan: Fleming H. Revell Co., 1984.

Wise, Robert L. *When There Is No Miracle.* Foreword by Rosalind Rinker. Ventura: Regal Books, 1977.

Yancey, Philip. *Helping the Hurting.* Portland: Multnomah Press, 1984.

Yancey, Philip. *Where Is God When It Hurts?* Grand Rapids: Zondervan Publishing House; Wheaton: Campus Life Books, 1977.